THE RESURRECTION LETTERS

THE RESURRECTION LETTERS

ST. ATHANASIUS

BISHOP OF ALEXANDRIA

FROM A.D. 328–373

PARAPHRASED AND INTRODUCED
BY
JACK N. SPARKS, Ph.D.

THOMAS NELSON PUBLISHERS
NASHVILLE

Scripture quotations within the Festal Letters are paraphrased from Athanasius' original translation. Unless otherwise indicated all other quotations are from *The New American Standard Bible*, © The Lockman Foundation 1960, 1962, 1963, 1968, 1971, 1972, 1973, 1975, and are used by permission.

 Published in Nashville, Tennessee by Thomas Nelson Inc., Publishers and simultaneously in Don Mills, Ontario, by Thomas Nelson & Sons (Canada) Limited. Manufactured in the United States of America.

Library of Congress Cataloging in Publication Data

Sparks, Jack N
The Resurrection letters, St. Athanasius, Bishop of Alexandria from 328–373.

1. Athanasius, Saint, Patriarch of Alexandria, d. 373. Epistolae festales. 2. Easter. I. Athanasius, Saint, Patriarch of Alexandria, Alexandria, d. 373. Epistolae festales. II. Title.
BR65.A443E6337 320'.1'40924 79-25102
ISBN 0-8047-5713-1

CONTENTS

Acknowledgments 9

PART I: ATHANASIUS, THE MAN AND HIS TIMES

About This Book 13
Easter in the Early Church 18
The Life of St. Athanasius 28

PART II: THE LETTERS

The First Letter, A.D. 329:
An Exhortation to a Proper Celebration
of This Proper Season

Introduction 46
Letter I 48

The Second Letter, A.D. 330:
Wickedness and Heresy

Introduction 58
Letter II 60

The Third Letter, A.D. 331:
Gratitude and Thanksgiving

Introduction 68
Letter III 70

The Fourth Letter, A.D. 332:
Passover Fulfilled in Christ the Lamb

Introduction 80
Letter IV 81

The Fifth Letter, A.D. 333:
Christ Satisfies Completely:
Respond Accordingly

Introduction 88
Letter V 90

The Sixth Letter, A.D. 334:
Glorify God With Your Body

Introduction 98
Letter VI 100

The Seventh Letter, A.D. 335:
Sinners Contrasted With the Righteous

Introduction 112
Letter VII 115

The Eighth Letter, A.D. 338:
Praise the Lord in Difficulties

Introduction 128
Letter VIII 130

The Ninth Letter, A.D. 339:
The Wicked Dig a Pit for Themselves

Introduction 144
Letter IX 146

The Tenth Letter, A.D. 341:
Suffering Prepares Us for Eternal Glory

Introduction 164
Letter X 166

The Eleventh Letter, A.D. 342:
Christ Is Our Holiness

Introduction 174
Letter XI 176

The Twelfth Letter, A.D. 347:
Be Strong in the Faith

Introduction 184
Letter XII 187

PART III: OUR RESPONSE

Let Us Celebrate the Feast 200
Suggested Readings for the Forty
Fast Days of Lent 203
Questions and Answers Concerning
Lenten Practices 205
Scripture Index 210
Subject and Name Index 217

ACKNOWLEDGMENTS

I owe a debt to many people in the preparation of this work, not least to my wife, Esther, and the deacons and presbyters who look after me daily. Ruth Berven did outstanding research on Easter, and I have utilized it freely. Linda Wallace (along with Madolyn Molloy), as ever, took my indecipherable scribblings and, by some sort of clerical transubstantiation, brought them through to manuscript form. Luanne Dunaway rendered invaluable assistance in preparing the indices. My fellow bishops—J. Richard Ballew, Kenneth A. Berven, Jon E. Braun, Peter E. Gillquist, and Gordon Thomas Walker encouraged and corrected me.

PART I

ATHANASIUS

THE MAN & HIS TIMES

ABOUT THIS BOOK

On many different occasions during the history of the church, God has raised up men of strong faith, stamina, and determination to save her from slipping into some ruinous heresy. St. Athanasius is just such a man. There arose in his time one of the most destructive of all heresies—Arianism, named after its chief proponent, Arius. Its main characteristic was the denial of the divinity of Jesus Christ.

From the beginning of the controversy, Athanasius was at the center of the storm that swirled throughout the church. He was archdeacon to Bishop Alexander of Alexandria when Arius first stubbornly set forth his error. He was spokesman for his bishop when the great Council of Nicaea (A.D. 325) was held to deal with the issue. And when Athanasius became bishop of Alexandria shortly thereafter, he became the focal point of the Arians' attack. Indeed, they often seemed on the verge of controlling the whole church in the decades that followed. Throughout Athanasius' lifetime the battle raged around him, so much so that it often seemed ridiculous that this one man should receive so much attention from the enemies of the church.

But there was good reason, as the life and work of this great man of God reveals. Athanasius understood how crucial was the doctrine of the divinity of the Son, and with great wisdom and understanding he refuted all the Arian arguments. But the genius of the man lay in his true holiness, his true devotion to the Lord, and his tenacious concern for the people of God. His was not a cold concern for the letter of orthodox doctrine. He had a real pastor's heart, and he knew that salvation depended upon God's being incarnate.

And so he spent his life battling this heresy, constantly harrassed, often in exile or in hiding, but still tenderly pastoring his flock as he was able. His efforts were not in vain, for in the end orthodoxy triumphed, and the faith was delivered from a horrible deception.

A CONTEMPORARY BEARS WITNESS

At the end of his life, St. Gregory Nazianzen, himself a great church figure of the fourth century, wrote an oration about his brother bishop. He wrote, in part:

> In praising Athanasius, I shall be praising virtue. To speak of him and to praise virtue are identical because he had, or actually, *has* thoroughly embraced virtue. I put it that way because all who have lived according to God still live to Him, though they have left life on this earth. After all, God is called the God of Abraham, Isaac, and Jacob because He is God not of the dead, but of the living.

A bit further on he wrote that Athanasius was . . .

> . . . distinguished in behavior and humble of mind. Unexcelled in virtue. Easily accessible for conversation. Gentle, free from anger, sympathetic. Kind in words and even kinder in disposition. Angelic in appearance but even more so in his way of thinking. Calm when delivering a rebuke and persuasive when he gave praise — not spoiling the effect of either by overdoing it — rebuking with the tenderness of a father and praising with the dignity of a ruler. His tenderness was not excessive nor his severity sour. On the one hand he was reasonable and on the other he was prudent, behaving very wisely. His bearing and character alone were adequate for training those who were his spiritual children, with very little need for words. And the words he did speak contained very little use of the rod (1 Cor. 4:21) and he seldom had to go so far as to use the knife in cutting away sin.

On Athanasius' theological leadership, Gregory said:

> [He was] aware that to compress the Three Persons into a numerical Unity is heretical, being the notión invented by Sabel-

> lius. He also knew that to sever the Three Persons from each other by saying that they differ in substance or nature is a horrible mutilation of Deity. Such knowledge and awareness enabled him to preserve the unity of the Godhead by consistently teaching the Trinity, dealing with the concept of person without either losing the Three Persons in the Unity or dividing the Substance among the Three Persons. . . . Therefore, he first helped stop the disease of heresy at the holy Council of Nicea, that gathering of the 318 chosen men united in the Holy Spirit. He was not yet one of the Bishops at that time, but he was held in the highest regard by the members of the Council because they considered virtue as valuable as office. Later, when the flame of heresy had been fanned by the blasts of the evil one and had become very widespread (so much so that almost the whole of earth and sea were enveloped in the resulting tragedies) the fight raged fiercely around him who was the noble champion of Christ the Word.

And a little further on:

> . . . when all the rest who sympathized with us were divided into three parties and many were faltering in their understanding of the Son and still more in that of the Holy Spirit, he was the first . . . to undertake to confess in writing, with absolute clarity and distinctness, the Unity of Godhead and Essence of the Three Persons. Thus he enabled us later under the influence of inspiration, to come to the same faith with respect to the Holy Spirit as most of the Fathers had already come to with respect to the Son.

Finally:

> He was the patron of the wedded and virgin state alike, both peaceable and a peacemaker, and an attendant upon those who are passing from this life. In fact, if I wanted to detail the excellence of his virtue, I would be able to confer many titles upon him.[1]

A MESSAGE FROM THE BISHOP

All these accolades and more are reflected in the warmth and

[1]Excerpted and paraphrased from *Oration* xxi, *On the Great Athanasius, Bishop of Alexandria*, Vol. 7, trans. Browne and Swallow, *A Select Library of Nicene and Post-Nicene Fathers of the Christian Church*, ed. Philip Henry Shaff and Henry Wace, Second Series (Grand Rapids: Eerdmans, 1974), pp. 269–280.

spirit of Athanasius' Festal Letters—his annual letters sent to the churches under his care, announcing the dates of Easter. Most of the letters also included a message to the people, exhorting and encouraging them, pointing them to the meaning of the Easter Feast. Each letter is packed with wisdom, knowledge, light, and blessing. They convey a sense of life with Christ and a participation in redemption that makes the heart of the believer leap with joy. Always Athanasius calls his people away from enchantment with the world to reality, from time to eternity.

In these days of light and frothy Christian books that fail to draw us to the heart of God, we have come to expect pop psychology and personal experience. Our diet of religious reading comes almost entirely from popular speakers, professors, fad promoters, and sociologists. What a pity! By missing the keen spiritual insight of the great Fathers of the faith, we are missing out on some of the best instruction the church has ever been given.

I first encountered the Festal Letters of St. Athanasius through my good friend, neighbor, and co-worker, Bishop J. Richard Ballew, who has spent thousands of hours studying the Council of Nicaea and the events and personalities surrounding it. Soon I longed to present those letters in the language of our day, and I have labored to do this faithfully. My prayer is that I have been able to adequately communicate Athanasius' messages.

I worked from the 1854 English translation by the Reverend Henry Burgess[2] and the revision of that translation by Miss Payne-Smith.[3] (Burgess made his translation from the Syriac version discovered a few years earlier.[4])

You will find twelve letters here; not all of Athanasius' Festal

[2]*The Festal Letters of St. Athanasius, Bishop of Alexandria* (London: Oxford University Press, 1854).

[3]*St. Athanasius: Select Works and Letters*, Vol. 4, *Nicene and Post-Nicene Fathers* (1971).

[4]I also found the Latin translations (*Patrum Nova Bibliotheca*, Tom. VI, Rome: Typis Sacri Consilii Propagando Christiano Nomini, 1853) to be useful in deciding on appropriate meanings for some expressions.

Letters are extant. These are the only ones we have in their entirety (with the exception of two which are very short, containing no message). In the older translation there are several fragments, but I have chosen to present only complete letters, because these set forth the full development of Athanasius' thought on his subject. These letters compose Part II of this volume.

Then, too, I have prepared a chapter on the life of Athanasius and a chapter on how Easter was celebrated in the early church. I trust these additions to Part I will help orient modern readers to the content of the letters. This book closes in Part III with a brief exhortation to the celebration of this greatest of all Christian holy days (we must be doers and not hearers only), together with a suggested schedule of pre-Easter readings and a review of Lenten practices in the church.

I therefore deliver these Festal Letters, these *Resurrection Letters*, with the hope and prayer that they will be of service to the church of Jesus Christ in these trying days, as they were in the trying days of their author.

JACK N. SPARKS
ACADEMY OF ORTHODOX THEOLOGY
ISLA VISTA, CALIFORNIA
APRIL, 1979

EASTER IN THE EARLY CHURCH

For most Americans the word "Easter" carries with it a variety of associations. Easter eggs (candy and painted). Candy in baskets. Bunnies. Baby chicks (marshmallow and real). Bright, new spring clothes. Parades. Ham for Sunday dinner. Oh yes—and Christ on and off the cross.

Those of us in the church know (as do probably most Americans) that the latter connection is the ancient one. Indeed, we would rate it as the most important association for us. At Easter we remember Christ on the cross, the empty tomb, and His resurrection. But what of our ancient predecessors in the faith? What did they believe? How did we arrive at today's celebration of Easter? The answers to these questions serve not only to inform us of the holy traditions of the early Christians, but they also set in vivid context the great importance of the *Resurrection Letters* of Athanasius.

A WORD WE NEED TO KNOW: *PASCHA*

From earliest Christian times, Easter has been *the most important* yearly festival of the church. It is, in fact, the oldest of all Christian celebrations.

As we go back to the beginning days of the church, we find that the church Fathers used a term unfamiliar to us for Easter —*Pascha*. A sermon for this great festival of the church, written by Melito of Sardis (c. 190), ends this way:

This is the alpha and the omega.
This is the beginning and the end—
an indescribable beginning
and an incomprehensible end.
This is the Christ.
This is the King.
This is the General.
This is the Lord.
This is the one who rose up from the dead.
This is the one who sits at the right hand of the Father.
He bears the Father
and is borne by the Father,
to whom be the glory
and the power forever. Amen.

The *Peri Pascha* of Melito:

Peace to the one who wrote,
and to the one who reads,
and to those who love the Lord
in simplicity of heart.[1]

But why the term *Pascha*? Because *Pascha* is the Aramaic derivation of the Hebrew word *Pesach,* which means "Passover." Most of the earliest Christians spoke Aramaic, and as the faith spread, the name was retained.

One thing we know for certain is that the church's origins are Jewish. It was to the Jews that the Messiah was promised, and it was to them that the Father sent the Son. The first apostles and Christians were Jews. And although the church quickly spread to the Gentile world and rapidly abandoned Jewish law and most Jewish customs, it began in a Jewish environment and was initially interpreted in this environment. We should not be surprised, therefore, that much Christian thought and practice is rooted in Judaism.

Thus the Pascha: Passover. Its very name is an arrow pointing down the long corridor of time, and its tip reaches to a slave people in Egypt.

[1]Gerald F. Hawthorne, "A New English Translation of Melito's Paschal Homily," *Current Issues in Biblical and Patristic Interpretation*, ed. Gerald F. Hawthorne (Grand Rapids: Eerdmans, 1975), pp. 174–75.

THE PASSOVER

The Passover was, and is, the major holiday (indeed, "holy day") in the Jewish calendar. It celebrates the Israelites' delivery out of slavery in Egypt. That deliverance is recorded in the second book written by Moses: Exodus. Most of us recall that event and the attendant circumstances. Israel had become a nation of slaves, building tombs, monuments, and cities for the great Pharaohs of Egypt. They might have remained there, eventually being assimilated into the local population. But God had a great destiny in mind for Israel, and He gave Moses the task of leading them out of Egypt.

But there was a problem. Pharaoh, king of Egypt, liked things as they were, and even a series of dreadful plagues sent by God was insufficient to move him. Finally God, through Moses, told each Israelite family to sacrifice a lamb and eat it hastily during the night, together with unleavened bread and certain herbs. They were to eat in traveling clothes, for they were about to leave. The blood of the lamb was to be put on the doorpost of every Israelite home. During that night the Lord killed the firstborn son of every Egyptian family, but the firstborn males of the Israelites were spared because of the blood on the doorposts.

So it was that Pharaoh gave up and allowed Israel to leave Egypt. This day of deliverance has been celebrated ever since. After the Exodus, God told Israel to keep a yearly Passover vigil, eating the sacrificial lamb, unleavened bread, and herbs during the night. They were to explain to their children the significance of the celebration, for, "It is a night to be observed for the LORD for having brought them out from the land of Egypt" (Exod. 12:42).

This is why we see that at the time of Christ every Jew made it a point to be in Jerusalem at least once in his life for the Passover, for it was only in Jerusalem that the Passover could be completely celebrated.

THE LITURGY

Each year, on the afternoon of the fourteenth of the Jewish

month Nisan,[2] the lambs brought by all Jews were slaughtered in the temple. Then each man would take his slaughtered lamb to his home or dwelling place to prepare for the supper that night. The Jewish day ran from sundown to sundown, so that very night was the fifteenth of Nisan, the night of the Passover. It was customary to fast on the fourteenth until the time of the Passover supper.

That supper was more than just a feast; it was a religious observance. Along with the actual meal there were blessings and prayers, psalms, and the reading and explanation of Scripture.

Each action of the Passover service had a meaning. All who partook, even the servants, were to recline while eating—the custom of the day for free men. Of course, the meal was eaten at night because it was during the night that the Lord had "passed over" His people. And every year Israel was to eat it in haste, dressed in traveling clothes, ready to "leave Egypt." The food, which included the Paschal sacrifice, unleavened bread, bitter herbs, and four glasses of wine, carried symbolic meaning. When the food was brought in, the eldest son was to ask his father why this night was different from all other nights.

Then the father instructed his son, reading the Passover story from Deuteronomy 26:5ff. and explaining it. Rabbi Gamaliel is quoted as saying that in order to fulfill the Passover, the verses concerning three things must be explained: "Passover, because God passed over the houses of our fathers in Egypt; unleavened bread, because our fathers were redeemed from Egypt; bitter herbs, because Egyptians embittered the lives of our fathers in Egypt." Then, following the explanation of Passover, after prayers and with the last glass of wine, the Hallel (Psalms 113–118) was sung.

MORE THAN A MEMORY

We must emphasize that *the Passover meant far more than a simple commemoration of the events of the Exodus*. For the

[2] The Jewish year begins with the month they call Nisan, which, because of calendar differences, falls somewhere between March and April.

people of Israel it was the great festival of redemption, and for the participants in the Passover supper there was a sense of *personal involvement* in that redemption. Indeed, the Mishna[3] says, "In every generation a man must so regard himself as if he came forth out of Egypt." Time was not a barrier to participation in that great deliverance. Each family member was instructed to view himself or herself as having been *personally* delivered by God from the hands of the Egyptian taskmasters. Part of the reenactment of the historical deliverance was also the expectation of future deliverance. The Passover was a feast of hope, looking forward to the coming of the Messiah.

OUR PASSOVER

To the church at Corinth, Paul the apostle wrote, "Christ, our Passover, was sacrificed for us. Therefore let us keep the feast" (1 Cor. 5:7). From the very beginning of the church Christ was clearly associated with the Passover lamb, and the supper immediately passed over into Christian practice. The Gospels and the Epistles tell us that the first Exodus finds its fulfillment in Jesus. Indeed, He speaks of Himself in terms of the Exodus and the Passover. The whole Gospel of John is built on the framework of the Passover and its celebration.

The annual celebration has a meaning centered on the risen Christ and the salvation accomplished in His death and resurrection. As St. Peter put it, the church is "a chosen generation, a royal priesthood, a holy nation, His own special people" (1 Peter 2:9). Thus there is good reason for St. Paul to tell the Christians at Corinth that Christ is the true Paschal Lamb who has been sacrificed for us (1 Cor. 5:7).

Just as the Jewish Passover celebration has the explanation built into it, so also the "royal priesthood" has the explanation, for in baptism its members have passed through the water, dying with Christ and rising in new life. St. Ambrose expressed well the concept of passage:

[3]This is the code of Jewish laws arranged about A.D. 200 which forms the foundation for the Talmud, the authoritative body of Jewish tradition.

> Now since you are celebrating the holy Pasch, you should know, brethren, what the Pasch is. Pasch means the *crossing-over*; and so the Festival is called by this name. For it was on this day that the children of Israel crossed over out of Egypt, and the Son of God crossed over from this world to His Father. What gain is it to celebrate the Pasch unless you imitate Him Whom you worship; that is unless you cross over from Egypt, that is, from the darkness of evildoing to the light of virtue, and from the love of this world to the love of your heavenly home?[4]

Although there were some variations in practice, the Pascha is most noted for the fact that the basic elements of its observance were the same everywhere.

THE PRECEDING FAST

Always the Paschal celebration was preceded by a fast. In the earliest days of the church, the service itself was an all-night vigil. It included the reading of Scripture, singing of Psalms, presentation of homilies, prayer, and baptism; and it concluded with a Eucharist.[5]

A *fast*? Yes, a fast! The church prepared itself for the festival, each one depriving the body that the whole person might be ready for the experience of redemption. It does not seem that the fast was the same everywhere, for early descriptions vary from fasts of one to six days. Nevertheless, a fast was common to all. By Athanasius' day in the fourth century, the fast extended over forty days, with those forty days associated closely with prayer, discipline, and good works — as well as the teaching of candidates for baptism. The days of Holy Week, leading up to the day of celebration, were special days of preparation.[6]

The Paschal observance began with a vigil on the Saturday night before Easter and continued until Sunday morning. But this vigil was not a preparation for a coming celebration; it was

[4] *Sunday Sermons of the Fathers*, (Chicago: Regnery Press, 1958), Vol. 3, p. 219.
[5] See, for example, *Didiscalia Apostolorum*, trans. R. H. Connolly (London: Oxford University Press, 1929), p. 189.
[6] For further information on fasting in the church, see the section in this book, "Questions and Answers Concerning Lenten Practices," p. 205.

in fact *the* celebration. Scripture portions on redemption were read, especially those of the Exodus. Interspersed among the readings were Psalms, chanted antiphonally, and homilies or sermons based on the various lessons. There was intercessory prayer for the lost and prayer for those about to be baptized. It seems that the Pascha was the most acceptable time of the year for new believers to be brought into the church — sometimes having waited as long as three years as "hearers of the Word"!

It should be emphasized that in all of these activities the thought was not simply on the commemoration of a past event; rather, it was an entering into it. Perhaps some words from a fourth-century sermon by John Chrysostom will help:

> I turn to those who in this blessed night are having the grace of baptism conferred on them: I address myself to those fair offshoots of the Church, those spiritual flowers, those new recruits of Jesus Christ. Two days ago the Lord died on the cross. Today he has risen from the dead. In the same way two days ago these neophytes were held in the bondage of sin. But today they rise along with Christ. He died in the flesh and rose in the flesh. They likewise were dead in sin and have risen from sin.[7]

THE FEAST

Then, finally, it was time for the Great Eucharist. The church remembered the night when it was delivered. The newly baptized joined the faithful at the Table of the Lord, and the night-long service was concluded with great joy and thanksgiving. In the morning the believers excitedly greeted each other, "Christ is risen!" to which the response was, "He is risen indeed!" The feasting was just beginning; the festival continued for fifty days following the Pascha, ending on Pentecost Sunday. Fasting and kneeling, which were forbidden on Sundays, were also forbidden during the season of Pentecost. It was a time of celebration for the church.

[7]Adelbert Hamman, ed., *The Paschal Mystery: Ancient Liturgies and Patristic Texts* (New York: Alba Books, 1969), p. 104.

THE MEANING OF IT ALL

Above all, in the early church the Paschal celebration was *the* celebration of our redemption. Just as today we see the Paschal lamb as a type or shadow of Christ, so also did the church fathers. They also saw the redemption of the Jews from Egypt as a prefiguring of our redemption from sin. Melito of Sardis said:

> For this one,
> Who was led away as a lamb,
> and who was sacrificed as a sheep,
> by himself delivered us from servitude to the world,
> as from the land of Egypt,
> and released us from bondage to the devil
> as from the hand of Pharaoh,
> and sealed our souls by his own spirit
> and the members of our bodies by his own blood.[8]
>
> This is the one who delivered us
> from slavery into freedom,
> from darkness into light,
> from death into life,
> from tyranny into an eternal kingdom,
> and who made us a new priesthood,
> and a special people forever.[9]

Baptism

Closely connected with this concept of redemption is the baptism of new believers, which was part of the celebration. Baptism was no light thing in the early church. As evidence we have St. Paul's statements in Romans 6:5,6:

> For if we have been united together in the likeness of His death, certainly we also shall be in the likeness of His resurrection, knowing this, that our old man was crucified with Him, that the body of sin might be done away with, that we should no longer serve sin.

[8]Hawthorne, *Current Issues*, pp. 164–65.
[9]*Ibid.*, p. 165.

And in Colossians 2:12:

> . . . buried with Him in baptism, in which you also were raised with Him through faith in the working of God, who has raised Him from the dead.

In baptism, a person is identified with Christ in His death and rises to a new life through Christ's resurrection. An early second-century document, *The Shepherd of Hermas*, says, "They go down into the water dead and they come up alive."[10] At the same time the believer is united with Christ, he is united to His body, the church. Again, from the apostle Paul we read:

> For by one Spirit we were all baptized into one body—whether Jews or Greeks, whether slaves or free, and have all been made to drink into one Spirit (1 Cor. 12:13).

Baptism, then, was no option to our church fathers. It was that act by which one died with Christ to the old way of life and rose with Him to a new life, a life united to Christ and to His body, the church. Since entrance into the redemption that the Pascha celebrates is tied to baptism, what better time to baptize those who believe? As a believer is submerged in the water, he is "buried with Christ," dead to sin and to the world. His rising up out of the water is a picture of his rising with Christ to a new life. For the early church this was not merely a symbol. In baptism they were actively experiencing their redemption. In an homily to newly baptized believers, Basil of Seleucia (A.D. 468) told them:

> . . . the Lord's body has been entrusted to you. More than that, I say you have become the body of the Lord, you are a member of Christ. In Paul's words, you have put on Christ: 'You have been baptized in Christ, you have put on Christ' "(Gal.3:27).[11]

[10]Jack Sparks, ed., *The Apostolic Fathers* (Nashville: Thomas Nelson, 1978), p. 246.
[11]Hamman, *Paschal Mystery*, p. 125.

The Eucharist

Indeed, the same is true of the Eucharist. The cup is a sharing in the blood of Christ and the bread is a sharing in the body of Christ (1 Cor. 10:16).

Thus, when the ancient church gathered for the Eucharist, it did not simply remember the historical events of the death and resurrection of Christ. No! These believers were partakers of the resurrected Lord. As Irenaeus of Lyons (c. 130–202), writing in defense of the redemption of the body, put it:

> For since we are his members, and are nourished by his creation—and he himself gives us this creation, making the sun to rise, and sending the rain as he wills—he declares that the cup, taken from the creation, is his own blood, by which he strengthens our blood, and he has firmly assured us that the bread, taken from the creation is his own body, by which our bodies grow. For when the mixed cup and the bread that has been prepared receive the Word of God, and become the Eucharist, the body and blood of Christ, and by these our flesh grows and is confirmed, how can they say that flesh cannot receive the free gift of God, which is eternal life, since it is nourished by the body and blood of the Lord and made a member of him. As the blessed Paul says in the Epistle to the Ephesians, that we are members of his flesh and his bones (Eph. 5:30).[12]

The early church lived in tension between two worlds (as do we, if we have not lost the vision). They saw themselves as living in the world, but at the same time as part of a kingdom that was not of the world—the kingdom Christ preached when He was on earth and which He would soon return to fully establish. In the meantime, the church lives in the world in time, but owes its allegiance to the Lord above time. In the Eucharistic meal, it all comes together in a looking back to the Lord's redemptive work, a present experiencing of the Lord's redemption and rule of His people, and a looking forward to His return to establish His kingdom in fullness.

[12]Cyril Richardson, "Irenaeus' *Against Heresies*," *Early Christian Fathers* (New York: Macmillan, 1970), p. 338.

THE LIFE OF ST. ATHANASIUS

It was perhaps an early summer evening in A.D. 313. Alexander, bishop of Alexandria in Egypt, waited in a beachside house for others to join him for dinner. Sitting relaxed by a window overlooking the shoreline, he observed a group of teen-aged boys playing on the beach.

Alexander soon realized that their play was not the typical roughhousing of adolescent boys; he was seeing a reenactment of certain aspects of the church's liturgy. Indeed, it became apparent that one of the boys was playing the role of bishop and that he was actually baptizing some of the others.

To the pious bishop this seemed just a bit too irreverent. Rising, he asked that the boys be brought in to him. When they appeared, awed and a bit frightened, he asked, "What were you boys doing out there?"

All looked to one slender youth, who was obviously going to be their spokesman.

"Sir," he said, "we were just playing."

"Didn't I see some of the baptismal liturgy?" inquired Alexander.

Young Athanasius was not at all eager to admit what had been going on. But Alexander pursued the matter, and finally Athanasius admitted, "Some of these fellows aren't in the church. I convinced them of Christ, and we baptized them."

"Don't you know better than to take such a responsibility on yourself?" Alexander asked.

"Y-yes sir!" was the stammering reply.

To his amazement, the bishop discovered that not only was the whole thing serious rather than a pretense, but all had been conducted according to the details of the baptismal liturgy. Since the boys obviously had faith in Jesus Christ, he was tempted to treat the baptisms as valid—and after talking it over with the other church leaders present, he did just that! Laying his own hands upon the heads of the newly baptized boys, Alexander confirmed their baptism.

HIS MINISTRY BEGAN

That was not the end of the matter. Messages were sent to the parents of the boy-bishop and the boys who were his "clergy" recommending that they be educated for the ministry. So it happened that Athanasius soon became the particular prodigy of the bishop.

During the next few years the young man's whole future was shaped. He was thoroughly educated in the Scriptures and the literature of the church. He learned languages and studied the Greek classics. But most of all, he learned practical theology as he served and studied at the side of Bishop Alexander, not living the "good life" of many modern scholars. The bishop, because of his love for Athanasius, gave his life discipline and order, for Alexander realized what we seem to have forgotten: Strong character is developed by facing difficulties, not by being sheltered from them.

Thus it was that at barely twenty years of age Athanasius produced a two-part work, *Against the Heathen* and *The Incarnation of the Word of God*. Anyone who has read these two books will agree that they deserve a place among the classics of Christianity. How could such a young man produce such valuable literature of the faith?

HIS TIMES

We must realize that Athanasius grew up in difficult times. It was in February, 303, before he was quite five years old, that the last great persecution was ordered by Emperor Diocletian.

From then until he was fourteen he was part of a church that knew a similar purge could happen again at any time. It did. In 311, the new Emperor Maximin ordered renewed persecution. The bishop of Alexandria was martyred, as were some who had been Athanasius' teachers. Close association with death and the immediate possibility of torture and martyrdom matured this young man far beyond his years.

According to Athanasius, these first two books were written specifically to teach a new believer by the name of Marcarius about the faith. Catch the simplicity of his expression. Athanasius was no speculative theologian or philosopher. His attitude is clearly represented by his concluding words to Marcarius:

> Here, then, Marcarius, is our offering to you who love Christ, a brief statement of the faith of Christ and of the manifestation of His Godhead to us. This will give you a beginning, and you must go on to prove its truth by the study of the Scriptures. They were written and inspired by God; and we, who have learned from inspired teachers who read the Scriptures and became martyrs for the Godhead of Christ, make further contribution to your eagerness to learn.
>
> From the Scriptures you will learn also of His second manifestation to us, glorious and divine indeed, when He shall come not in lowliness but in His proper glory, no longer in humiliation but in majesty, no longer to suffer but to bestow on us all the fruit of His cross — the resurrection and incorruptibility. No longer will He then be judged, but rather will Himself be Judge, judging each and all according to their deeds done in the body, whether good or ill. Then for the good is laid up the heavenly kingdom, but for those that practise evil outer darkness and the eternal fire. So also the Lord Himself says, "I say unto you, hereafter ye shall see the Son of Man seated on the right hand of power, coming on the clouds of heaven in the glory of the Father." For that Day we have one of His own sayings to prepare us, "Get ready and watch, for ye know not the hour in which He cometh." And blessed Paul says, "We must all stand before the judgment seat of Christ, that each one may receive according as he practised in the body, whether good or ill."[1]

[1]*St. Athanasius on the Incarnation* (Crestwood, N.Y.: St. Vladimir's Press, 1977), p. 95.

A GIFT OF DISCERNMENT

You see something here that is prominent throughout the life and teaching of Athanasius. He knew salvation was through Christ, and that if one doesn't believe in the *right* Christ, he will miss that salvation.

Soon Athanasius was a deacon, and then head of all the deacons of Alexandria — the archdeacon. He remained a close associate and right-hand servant to his bishop.

Those were hard years for Bishop Alexander. In 319, he first faced a heresy that was to disturb the whole church for half a century and would absorb the whole life of his young deacon. In 319 a presbyter named Arius first began to teach of Christ: "There was a time when He was not." And the war was on.

Athanasius was by Alexander's side when the bishop pleaded with Arius to repent; when Alexander called a council in Egypt, by which Arius was denounced and deposed; when the great ecumenical council of 325 convened at Nicaea to deal with the issue that now disturbed the whole church.

A letter by Alexander gives a clear picture of the problem.

> The novelties they [Arius and his followers] have invented and put forth contrary to the Scriptures are these following:
>
> (1) God was not always a Father, but there was a time when God was not a Father.
> (2) The Word of God [Christ the Son] was not always, but originated from things which were not; for God who is has made Him who was not, out of that which was not; therefore there was a time when He was not; for the Son is a creature and a work; neither is He like in substance to the Father.
> (3) Neither is He the true and natural Word of the Father; neither is He His true Wisdom; but He is one of the things made and created, and is called the Word and Wisdom by an abuse of terms, since He Himself originated by the proper Word of God, and by the Wisdom that is in God, by which God has made not only all other things, but Him also.
> (4) Therefore He is by nature subject to change and variation, as are all rational creatures.

(5) The Word is foreign from the substance of the Father and is alien and separated from it.
(6) The Father cannot be described by the Son, for the Word does not know the Father perfectly and accurately, neither can He see Him perfectly.
(7) Moreover the Son does not know His own essence as it really is; for He is made for us that God might create us by Him, as by an instrument; and He would not have existed had not God wished to create us.

Accordingly, when someone asked them whether the Word of God can possibly change, as the devil changed, they were not afraid to say that He can; for being something made and created, His nature is subject to change.[2]

AT NICAEA

At the Nicaean Council, the young Archdeacon Athanasius from Alexandria distinguished himself by his powerful refutation of Arian spokesmen. He was there, triumphant and enthusiastic, when on June 19, 325, the Creed of the Council was signed:

> We believe in one God the Father All-sovereign, maker of all things visible and invisible; and in one Lord Jesus Christ, the Son of God, begotten of the Father, only begotten, that is, of the substance of the Father, God of God, Light of Light, true God of true God, begotten not made, of one substance with the Father, through whom all things were made, things in heaven and things on earth; who for us men and for our salvation came down and was made flesh, and became man, suffered, and rose on the third day, ascended into the heavens, is coming to judge living and dead. And in the Holy Spirit. And those that say: "There was when he was not," and "Before he was begotten he was not," and that, "He came into being from what is not," or those that allege that the Son of God is: "Of another substance or essence" or "created," or "changeable," or "alterable," these the Catholic and Apostolic Church anathematizes.

As Athanasius journeyed home with his bishop, the issue

[2]From "Deposition of Arius," *St. Athanasius: Select Works and Letters*, Vol. 4, A *Select Library of Nicene and Post-Nicene Fathers of the Christian Church*, ed. Philip Schaff and Henry Wace, Second Series (Grand Rapids: Eerdmans, 1971), p. 70.

seemed settled. Most of the Arian spokesmen were in exile, and with a Christian emperor, peace seemed certain for the church.

There was peace for a while. Things were quiet in Alexandria when Alexander died in the spring of 328. It seemed that everyone wanted Athanasius to be the new bishop, although he was barely thirty. Besides, he was the choice of his predecessor.

It was therefore no surprise that when the bishops of Egypt and Libya met to choose the new bishop, their choice was Athanasius. On June 8, 328, he was consecrated to the office.

THE OCCASION OF THE LETTERS

It was the annual custom of the bishop of Alexandria to prepare a "Festal Letter," or Easter Letter, to give the dates of the fast before Easter and also the date of Easter itself. But the letter was also a message of teaching, encouragement, and exhortation to the flock. In his first Easter Letter, Athanasius wrote, in part:

> We are purified by His precious blood, which cleanses us from sin. His blood does not cry out for vengeance as did the blood of Abel (Heb. 12:24). Our feet are shod with the preparation of the gospel (Eph. 6:15), and we carry the rod and staff of the Lord, our Shepherd. We are comforted, as was the one who said, "Thy rod and Thy staff they comfort me" (Ps. 23:4).
>
> Collectively, then, as the people of God, we are completely prepared for whatever comes and do not have to worry about anything. The apostle Paul wrote, "The Lord is at hand" (Phil. 4:5). And our Savior Himself told us that He will come when He is not expected (Luke 12:40).
>
> So, "Let us keep the feast, not with old leaven, neither with the leaven of malice and wickedness, but with the unleavened bread of sincerity and truth" (1 Cor. 5:8). "Putting off the old man and his deeds, let us put on the new man" (Eph. 4:22–24), which is created in God, in humbleness of mind and a pure conscience. Indeed, let us meditate on His law by day and by night. Also, let us rid ourselves of all hypocrisy and fraud, and free ourselves of haughtiness and deceit. Then let us take up love towards God and neighbor. Thus prepared as new creatures drinking the new wine —the Holy Spirit—we will be able to properly keep the Feast, the season of these new fruits (from *Festal Letter* I).

This excerpt typifies the lifelong attitude of this man, who focused on redemption and the life of the redeemed. Indeed, the reason for his unswerving insistence upon orthodoxy concerning Christ was the sure knowledge that salvation itself is at stake.

During the next several years, the young bishop devoted himself to the zealous care of his flock. His zeal for Christ was infectious, and the church's devotion to the Lord and His body was at a high point in Egypt. Widows and orphans received care, and the church grew.

ARIANS REAPPEAR

But the enemies of Christ were not at rest. They concocted a variety of schemes and allegations in attempts to depose Athanasius. He cleared himself time and time again, once in a personal appearance before the emperor. The Arians were most persistent, however, and they finally prevailed upon Constantine to command Athanasius to appear at a council in Tyre. There, in 335, all the old charges were renewed and again proven false. New ones were also brought; for example, Athanasius was charged with cutting off a man's hand.

The Arian accusers brought in a box, which was opened and paraded before the whole council amid gasps of horror. In that box was a hand which, they explained, Athanasius had taken from a man named Arsenius, murdering him in the process. Further, Athanasius had used the hand for magical purposes.

But Athanasius had gotten wind of this plot well ahead of time and had managed to locate and trace the movements of this Arsenius, who was very much alive. When the hand was produced, he asked his accusers, "Did you know Arsenius personally?"

From several the reply was prompt and eager, "Oh yes, certainly."

So Athanasius had Arsenius brought in, wrapped in a cloak, and they had to agree that it was he. Then, as the council waited expectantly for an explanation of how his hand had been lost, Athanasius turned back the man's cloak to show that at least one hand was still there. Then, as the whole council waited in breathless anticipation, he turned back Arsenius' other sleeve. There was a second hand! Now Athanasius took advantage of the shock. "Where," he inquired, "did he grow the third hand which you have in the box?"

THE YEARS OF EXILE

Nothing, however, was going to deter the Arians from their aim. They brought more charges, which Athanasius knew would require investigation, and he knew what he had to do: He had to see the emperor. Along with four Egyptian bishops, he left Tyre secretly and sailed to Constantinople.

There he requested an audience with Constantine, which the dumbfounded emperor granted.

Meanwhile, the Arians had excluded all testimony but their own on another of their ridiculous charges, and the council had deposed Athanasius. The Arian accusers left for Jerusalem, but they were immediately summoned to Constantinople to appear for Athanasius' hearing. There they blithely changed their whole approach and tossed up a brand new charge: Athanasius, they said, had prevented the sailing of grainships from Alexandria to the capital city. That hit Constantine where he lived, and without even investigating the charge he exiled the great bishop to Treves in Gaul. Athanasius left on February 8, 336.

There is no record of an Easter Letter to Athanasius' flock in the years 336 and 337, so we do not know whether he wrote any or not. While he was gone, Arius died, but there was no weakening of the strength of the heretics. Constantine also died and was succeeded as emperor by his sons, Constantine II, Constans, and Constantius. Constantius, emperor in the East, allowed Athanasius to return on November 23, 337.

The attitude of the good bishop during his exile is reflected in his Easter Letter of 338:

> Although I committed all my affairs to God, I still wanted to celebrate the Feast with you, disregarding the distance between us. For although distance separates us, the Lord who gives the

> Feast is the Feast (1 Cor. 5:7). He bestows the Spirit, bringing us together in mind, in harmony, and in the bond of peace (from *Festal Letter* VIII).

Back in Alexandria, the storm had not abated. The Arians had sent a man named Pistus to take over as bishop during the absence of Athanasius. However, this man commanded no following, and nothing came of his appointment. Meanwhile, Athanasius called the Egyptian bishops together and composed a letter dealing thoroughly with all the weak charges the Arian bishops had made against him. Athanasius was reinstated. But the Arians were not finished. They called a council at Antioch and again deposed Athanasius, sending a man named Gregory to take his place. This man, backed by a pagan governor, instituted a reign of terror among the Christians in the city. Athanasius escaped and sailed for Rome on April 16, 339.

This time it would be more than seven years before Alexandria saw its beloved bishop. The city of Rome, however, was undoubtedly greatly influenced by this man. He was not just theologically orthodox; he also lived and breathed his personal intimacy with Jesus Christ, Son of God and Son of man.

Emperor Constantius proved to be an Arian sympathizer, so in the east the Arians made great headway. However, they pulled so many disgusting tricks that even Constantius became disenchanted with them. Besides, his brother Constans threatened war if Athanasius were not allowed to return. So Athanasius received a letter from Constantius asking him to come back home!

From the Easter Letters he wrote in exile, one can see that Athanasius kept his flock continually in mind. From Rome, his letter of 341 contained these words:

> We have indeed experienced numerous attacks and much bitter persecution aimed at the church. Heretics, unfamiliar with the faith and corrupt in their thinking, have risen up against the truth and are violently persecuting the church. Some of the brothers and sisters have been whipped and others have been torn apart on the rack. This ill treatment has become so vicious that it has even spread to the bishops. Nevertheless, it is not appropriate for us to neglect the Feast because of such things (from *Festal Letter* X).

THE GOLDEN DECADE

Back home once again, Athanasius experienced what has been called the "golden decade" of his life. When he arrived on October 21, 346, a great celebration took place. People met him as far away as a hundred miles from the city. Thus began his longest uninterrupted term in the office of bishop. His return brought a great revival in Alexandria; widows and orphans were fed and clothed, there was great peace in the churches of Egypt, and the quality of life in general was raised.

During these years Athanasius gathered the necessary materials to write his major book, *Apology Against the Arians*, as well as other valuable works. His deep sense of the value of our redemption is reflected in a preserved fragment of his Easter Letter of 348:

> Let us now keep the Easter Feast, brothers and sisters. For as our Lord reminded His disciples of Passover, He reminds us that Passover will be here in a few days (cf. Matt. 26:2). On that Passover the Jews betrayed the Lord, but we celebrate His death as a Feast, for because of it we were delivered from our afflictions. Yes, and though we were scattered, now we assemble eagerly together; though we were lost, we have been found; though we were far from Him, we have been brought near; though we were strangers, we have become His. For He suffered for us, and was nailed on the cross. As the prophet says (Isa. 53:4), He bore our sins and was afflicted for us in order to take away all our grief, sorrow, and mourning. When we are thirsty, He brings us to the Feast and satisfies us, as He promised when He stood and cried, "If anyone is thirsty, let him come to Me and drink" (John 7:37).

Constantius became ruler of the whole Roman Empire in 350. The Arians had not forgotten their enemy; they knew that as long as Athanasius was bishop in Alexandria they could never take over the whole church. Indeed, even their present holdings were not safe.

In 353 and 355, councils were held at Arles and Milan, respectively, and the emperor forced the attending bishops, under pain of exile, to sign condemnations of Athanasius. Many orthodox bishops were exiled, and a government official arrived in Alexandria in January, 356, to take Athanasius. The people protested, and Athanasius held a great final service with Psalm 136 recited, the people responding after each verse, "for His mercy endureth forever."

THE ESCAPE

The beloved bishop escaped the hands of the soldiers and went into the Egyptian desert, lost from public view for six years and fourteen days. It seemed that Arianism had finally triumphed, but it was really going down for the third time. Athanasius never left Egypt; in fact, he was often in Alexandria itself. And although the government bitterly persecuted the people, the man the Arians had appointed bishop was never able to take full charge.

Athanasius continued to write, primarily against the Arians, but also on the coessentiality of the Holy Spirit—an important topic in view of future developments. He also continued to guide the churches. In the meantime, the emperor's soldiers searched for him frantically but futilely.

This alone is testimony to three important facts. First, it is a testimony to the loyalty and devotion of the people of God, who successfully hid and protected their bishop during this entire period. Secondly, the love, sovereignty, and power of God is visibly displayed by the very fact that this champion of the truth remained alive and safe through all those years in which his life was in jeopardy. And third, it is a testimony to the character of Athanasius. He was no fearful weakling, but a man of great moral fiber — not soft and flabby physically, mentally, or spiritually. He was a bright and vivid man of strong conviction, committed totally to the providence of God. Never did he shrink from speaking the truth.

In his letter to the bishops of Egypt, written during this period, he wrote:

> [The Lord said] "Beware of false prophets, which come to you in sheep's clothing, but inwardly they are ravening wolves" (Matt. 7:15) and [spoke] by the mouth of His holy Apostles,

"Believe not every spirit" (1 John 4:1). That is the way our adversaries operate. All these heretical novelties are like that; they all have the devil as the father of their subtleties. And remember, he changed and became a liar and a murderer back in ages past. But since they are ashamed to claim his [the devil's] hateful name, they usurp the glorious Name of our Savior "which is above every name." They deck themselves out in the language of Scripture, saying the words, but robbing them of their true meaning. Thus, disguising their false intentions by some trick, they become the murderers of those whom they have led astray.[3]

REAFFIRMATION OF NICAEA

In November, 361, Constantius died. Julian, a pagan, had already taken power in the West, and he now became sole emperor. One of his first acts was to recall all the bishops exiled by Constantius, and on February 21, 362, Athanasius appeared openly in Alexandria. There he held a godly council in Alexandria to deal with how to restore peace in the church. That council was the crowning achievement of his life, and it led to great unity in the church and a reaffirmation of the Nicaean Creed.

One great accomplishment of this council was the clearing up of misunderstandings that had arisen from differing uses of the Greek word *hypostasis* (essence or substance). Through the wise guidance of Athanasius, the whole matter was thoroughly discussed. Both parties agreed that they believed the same thing and both endorsed the Creed of Nicaea.[4]

But Julian, openly espousing his paganism, was afraid of Athanasius' power in Egypt. He ordered him out, and again the venerable saint had to flee for his life, this time on October 23, 362. Prophesying Julian's soon demise, he said, "Be of good heart; it is only a cloud, and will soon pass away."

It was during this exile that Athanasius, heading up the Nile in a boat, heard that government soldiers were not far behind. He had the boat turned around and soon met his pursuers. Not knowing to

[3]Paraphrased from *St. Athanasius: Select Works and Letters*, p. 224.
[4]For a full and interesting account, see "Synodal Letter to the People of Antioch," *ibid.*, pp. 483–486.

whom he spoke, the leader of the pursuit called across to Athanasius, "Have you any news of Athanasius?"

The good bishop himself gave the reply, "He is not far off."

The boats passed without further incident.

When Julian died the next summer, Athanasius went to see Jovian, the new emperor, at Edessa. He left with an imperial letter restoring him as bishop of Alexandria. Again he resumed his efforts on behalf of the church—locally and everywhere. He had hardly arrived home when Jovian died from inhaling the fumes of a charcoal fire at a wayside inn.

ONE LAST EXILE

An army officer named Valentinian became emperor, and he gave the eastern half of the empire to his brother, Valens. The latter soon fell under the influence of Arians, and that heresy thereby had its last major thrust. Once again an order was sent out to expel Athanasius. By now the people were most exasperated with the repeated harrassment of their bishop, and riots broke out. Athanasius left town ahead of the imperial officers and again hid near Alexandria. But this was a short exile. He left on October 5, 365, and the unrest of the people brought his recall on February 1, 366.

Thus Athanasius was back from his fifth and last exile. He cared for his flock and continued to write, although most of the writing in his old age was contained in letters dealing with doctrinal topics. Two of his last works were against the views of Apollinaris, who had once been his close friend. Apollinaris had begun to teach that Christ took a body with *soul*, but that the place of the human *spirit* was taken by the *Word* (the divine person of the Son), thus leaving the Incarnation incomplete. Athanasius, aware of the relationship of salvation to the nature of Christ, could not let such an error pass.

THE FINAL YEARS

Time passed, and Athanasius, undoubtedly feeling the weight of old age, looked forward more and more to his eternal home. His Easter Letter of 371 quotes the Letter to the Hebrews: " 'For we have here no abiding city, but we seek that which is to come.' " By 373, Athanasius had been bishop for forty-five years, spending almost twenty of those years in exile. In a surviving fragment of his Easter Letter of that year, we find these words:

> . . . whereas we were once strangers, we are called friends; though we were formerly aliens, we have become fellow citizens with the saints, and are called children of the heavenly Jerusalem, that great city of which the one Moses built is a picture. For if Moses made everything according to the pattern shown him in the mountain, then the worship and service carried out in the tabernacle was a type of the heavenly mysteries. And the Lord, wanting us to enter that heavenly city, prepared a new and permanent way for us to do so. And, just as all those ancient Mosaic practices were types or shadows of the new, so our present Easter Festival is a type of the joy of heaven. Therefore, let us begin the pre-Easter fasts with psalms and spiritual songs, aiming joyfully for the Feast to come.

So on May 2, 373, this great hero of the faith (wrote a contemporary), "departed this life in a wonderful manner." Amen.

PART II

THE LETTERS

THE FIRST LETTER

A.D. 329

AN EXHORTATION TO A PROPER CELEBRATION OF THIS PROPER SEASON

INTRODUCTION TO THE FIRST LETTER

Athanasius became bishop in 328, and his first Easter Letter was written the following year. The tone of his episcopal ministry is set right away, as he issues a trumpet call to the highest holy day of Christendom. On this particular Easter he urges his flock to celebrate the day because it is specifically set aside by God. He wants no mistake about the fact that this is not some humanly chosen day. It is the Christian Passover, given by God.

But that isn't all. He writes of the preparatory fast—and he gets tough! Yes, one should abstain from food, for that is appropriate in preparing one's heart and mind for the celebration. At the same time, however, he makes it abundantly clear that a mere ritual abstention from food has no inherent worth. Better, give attention to being right in your heart and behaving in an upright manner. "Many people," he points out, "though they go through the motions of a fast, are still polluted in their hearts because they do evil against their brothers and sisters or because they dare to cheat."

Both of these points need to be heard by the church in our day. Many, it seems, do not have a heartfelt grasp of the season as holy unto the Lord, or of Easter as that Great Eucharist of the year. We, too, need to hear the exhortation of the apostle Paul: "Christ, our Passover, was sacrificed for us. Therefore let us keep the feast, not with old leaven, nor with the leaven of malice and wickedness" (1 Cor. 5:7,8).

Fasting as a holy exercise seems to be out of fashion today. In fact, most people think of fasting only as a way to lose weight. Too many who fast during this season or any other do it simply as an exercise of obligation. There is no self-examination or penitence involved in their fasts. But worst of all, holy thoughts and actions are seldom attached to fasting these days.

Things can and should be different, however. Remember what St. James wrote: "Pure and undefiled religion is this: to visit orphans and widows in their trouble, and to keep oneself unspotted from the world" (James 1:27).

LETTER I

A.D. 329

Come, dear brothers and sisters. We are nearing the season of the Easter Feast. Once again "the Sun of Righteousness" (Mal. 4:2) reminds us that the day of celebration of Easter is coming. If we celebrate it, in obedience to Him, then after it's all over we will be happy. For it is our duty and obligation to remember and heed the day every year, just as St. Paul taught his disciple Timothy to be aware of dates, saying, "Stand ready in season, and out of season" (2 Tim. 4:2).

Paul wrote that, of course, so that Timothy would do things when they were supposed to be done and avoid the blame for doing things at the wrong time. In the same way, the God of all has set times and seasons for everything (Eccles. 3:1), so that in due time salvation would be brought to people everywhere.

GOD KNOWS THE RIGHT TIME

Thus, for instance, at the right time—not the wrong time—the "Wisdom of God" (1 Cor. 1:24), our Lord and Savior Jesus Christ, "passed into holy souls, making them friends of God, and prophets."[1] Very many people were praying for the coming of Christ, saying with the psalmist, "O that the salvation of God would come out of Zion!" (Ps. 14:7) and praying as the spouse did in Solomon's Song, "O that you were like a brother to me, that nursed at my mother's breasts" (Song of Solomon 8:1). And

[1]Wisdom 7:27.

the meaning of that prayer is, "O that *you* were like human beings and would take on human nature for our sake." After all, it was God who set up times and seasons, and He knows our needs better than we do. Because He loves us, He exhorts us to do right things at right times so that we may be healed. Thus, when the appropriate time came, the Father sent the Son, just as He had promised through Isaiah the prophet, "In a favorable time I have answered you, and in the day of salvation I have helped you" (Isa. 49:8). For the same reason, the blessed apostle Paul, urging us to keep Easter—this season of the feast of our salvation — wrote: "Behold, now is the accepted time, behold, now is the day of salvation" (2 Cor. 6:2).

THE LORD'S TRUMPET CALL

Back in Old Testament days the Lord called Israel to festivals (one of which, brothers and sisters, is now at hand) at certain times of the year: "Three times a year you shall celebrate a feast to me" (Exod. 23:14). The people were called to these celebrations by the blowing of trumpets with great ceremony. The psalmist, for example, gave the command, "Blow the trumpet at the new moon, at the full moon, on our feast day" (Ps. 81:3). Sometimes the trumpets called the people to celebration, sometimes to fasting, and sometimes to war. Always the call was solemn and serious, because none of these matters are commonplace. Yes, the call of the trumpet was reserved for serious occasions so that the people would come together when called.

You don't have to take my word for it, for the Scriptures tell us, "And the Lord spoke to Moses, saying, Make yourself two trumpets of silver, of hammered work you shall make them; and you shall use them for summoning the congregation" (Num. 10:1). All of this was for the time of Moses and indeed, as long afterward as the Lord dealt with Israel in preparation for the coming of the Savior. It all had to do with properly following the Lord "till the time of reformation" (Heb. 9:10). For the Lord said, "When you go to war in your land against the adversary who attacks you [for these commands have to do with the promised land, and nothing more], then you shall sound an alarm with the trumpets, that you may be remembered before the Lord your God, and be saved from your enemies" (Num. 10:9).

But they did not blow the trumpet only in wars. Under the law there was also a festal trumpet. In that same passage we read, "Also in the day of your gladness and in your appointed feasts, and on the first days of your months, you shall blow the trumpets" (Num. 10:10). This instruction about the trumpets is no light or silly matter; it is actually a wonderful and awesome thing. Israel was given instruction by means of trumpets because their blasts are exciting and terrifying. In its infant stages Israel needed that.

In order that the proclamation should not be seen as merely human, the Lord ordered trumpet blasts that reminded the people of the shock of those voices they heard on Mount Sinai (Exod. 19:16). Thus, after being reminded of the Law they had been given, they kept it. After all, the Law *was* worthy of admiration and the picture of what was to come *was* excellent. That was why those who heard the trumpet blasts felt fear and reverence, especially those who had not only heard the sounds on the mountain but had also seen the signs God gave.

THE CHRISTIAN TRUMPET

Well, then, all those things were pictures foreshadowing what was to come. Let us, then, leave them behind and turn our minds to that which they portrayed. Consider the "priestly trumpets" of our Savior that sometimes call us to war, as the apostle Paul said: "For our struggle is not against flesh and blood, but against the rulers, against the powers, against the world-forces of this darkness, against the spiritual forces of wickedness in the heavenly places" (Eph 6:12). Sometimes the call is to virginity, or to humility, or to marital harmony; thus God might call virgins to the things of virgins, and those who have vowed to abstain to the things of abstinence, and those who are married to the things of an honorable marriage. Thus each maintains his own virtues and his own rewards.

On the other hand, sometimes the call is to fasting, and

sometimes to a feast. Listen to the apostle Paul again "blowing the trumpet," and proclaiming, "Christ our Passover has been sacrificed; let us therefore keep the feast, not with old leaven, nor with the leaven of malice and wickedness" (1 Cor. 5:7,8).

And there is an even greater trumpet than all of these—our Savior. "On the last day, the great day of the feast, Jesus stood and cried out, saying, 'If any man is thirsty, let him come to me and drink' " (John 7:37). For the Savior did not just call us to *a* feast, but to *the Great Feast*, because He wants us to be prepared to hear and obey every true trumpet call of God.

THE CHARACTER OF A REAL FAST

Since, as I said, there are many kinds of proclamations, let us listen to the trumpet blast of the prophet: "Blow a trumpet in Zion, consecrate a fast" (Joel 2:15). This is a warning trumpet, and it earnestly commands us that when we fast, we should do it in a holy manner, for God is holy and has pleasure in His holy people (Ps. 16:3). Not everyone, however, who calls upon God honors Him. Some defile Him—although they don't actually defile *Him*: that's impossible. But they *do* defile their own consciences concerning Him.

The apostle Paul tells us how it is that some people dishonor God: Those who break the Law dishonor God (Rom. 2:23). So the prophet said, in order to point out those who pollute the fast, "Sanctify a fast." Many people, though they go through the motions of a fast, are still polluted in their hearts because they do evil against their brothers and sisters or because they dare to cheat. And many, if nothing else, think more highly of themselves than of their neighbors, thereby committing a great offense.

Remember the story the Lord told of the Pharisee who fasted twice each week (Luke 18:10). His fasting did him no good, simply because he considered himself better than the publican. In the same manner the Lord found fault with the children of Israel because they had that kind of attitude in their fast and then made a great pretense of humility: "Is it a fast like this which I choose, a day for a man to humble himself? Is it for bowing one's head like a reed, and for spreading out sack cloth and ashes as a bed? Will you call this a fast, even an acceptable day to the Lord?" (Isa. 58:5).

In order to see what we should be like when we fast, and what the fast should be like, listen to what God told Moses: "On exactly the tenth day of this seventh month is the day of atonement; it shall be a holy convocation for you, and you shall humble your souls and present an offering by fire to the Lord" (Lev. 23:26).

FOOD OF THE SOUL

A little further on He makes the issue very clear: "If there is any person who will not humble himself on this same day, he shall be cut off from his people" (Lev. 23:29). See then, brothers and sisters, what a real fast amounts to, and how we are supposed to fast. We are not to fast only with the body, but also with the soul. Now the soul is humbled when it is not occupied with wicked ideas, but is fed by appropriate thoughts.

Virtues and vices are the food of the soul and it can feed on either one, turning to whichever one it wants to. If it is bent toward moral excellence, it will be fed by virtue — by righteousness, temperance, meekness, endurance. In other words, it's just as St. Paul says, "being nourished by the word of truth" (1 Tim. 4:6). That's the way it was with our Lord, who said, "My food is to do the will of Him who sent Me" (John 4:34).

But if the soul does not incline toward good things, but rather toward evil, it is nourished by nothing but sin. The Holy Spirit, describing sinners and their food, alluded to the devil when he said, "Thou didst give him as food for the people of the wilderness" (Ps. 74:14). Our Lord and Savior Jesus Christ is heavenly bread, the food of the saints, as He said: "Unless you eat My flesh, and drink My blood" (John 6:53). In the same way, the devil is the food of impure people who want nothing to do with the light, but want to do the works of darkness. Therefore, in order to turn His people away from vices, God commands them to feed on virtue, which is humbleness of mind, willingness to endure humiliation, and the acknowledgment of God.

FASTING IS A PREPARATION

Fasting like this not only makes God look on us favorably, but it also prepares us for the Easter Feast by setting our hearts on things above. Consider the facts written in the Scriptures about great men of old. Moses was fasting when he talked with God and received the Law. That very great and holy man Elijah, when fasting, was thought worthy of divine vision. At the end of his life he was taken up like the Lord, who ascended into heaven. Daniel, too, though a very young man, was entrusted with things no one else knew while he was fasting. He was made to understand the king's problems and was given divine visions.

Now, no one should be skeptical of the fact that these men often fasted for very long periods of time. We need to understand that looking to God and the word that proceeds from Him is enough nourishment for those who hear. It takes the place of all food. Do not forget that the angels are sustained by looking at all times on the face of the Father—and of the Savior who is in heaven. So Moses could fast bodily as long as he talked with God, for he was nourished by divine words. But when he came down from the presence of God to live among other people, he got hungry just as they did. That is why he fasted for just the forty days during which he talked with God. And many of the saints have had a similar experience.

THE JEWS MISUNDERSTAND

Therefore, brothers and sisters, let us nourish our souls with divine food, Jesus Christ the Word. And, fasting with both body and soul as God desires, let us keep this great and saving fast as we should. Even the Jews, foolish as they were, actually received a type of this divine food when they ate the Passover lamb. Although they no longer have the city (Jerusalem) nor the truth, they still eat the lamb, even to this day, without understanding the type. As long as Judea and Jerusalem existed, they were a picture and a type of a lamb. But the Law commanded that the sacrifices should not be carried on anywhere else.

Further, the Law commanded them to build their altar and their temple in Jerusalem—and in Jerusalem *only*. Therefore, the whole burnt offerings and sacrifices were to be offered only there, so that when that city came to an end, these figurative things would also come to an end. Now consider: After the coming of the Savior, that city was destroyed and the whole land of Judea was laid waste. Thus, the Jewish sacrificial system also ended.

Again, you don't just have my word for it. The prophet Nahum proclaimed the good news of what was to come, "Behold upon the mountains the feet of him who brings good news, who announces peace" (Nah. 1:15). Then he went on to tell them, "Celebrate your feasts, O Judah; pay your vows. For they shall no more go to that which is old; it is finished; it is taken away: he is gone up who breathed upon the face, and delivered you from affliction" (Nah. 1:15; 2:1).

THE JEWISH ORDINANCES ENDED

Now who is he who went up? Notice, by the way, that the one who went up went to the Jews, so there is no way they can ignore the end of those practices that foreshadowed His coming. And the prophet did say, "It is finished." But as I asked, who was he? It would be absurd to say that he was Moses, because when he was with Israel they hadn't even entered the land in which these sacrificial rites were to be carried out. Or suppose that he was Samuel or some other one of the prophets. That wouldn't do either, because while they were around the sacrifices were being made and Jerusalem was still standing. Thus it was none of these men who went up.

But if you want to know the truth and not some Jewish fable, look to our Savior, who went up and who "breathed upon them, and said to them, 'Receive the Holy Spirit' " (John 20:22). As soon as these things were done, all the old things came to an end. The altar was broken; the veil of the temple was torn from top to bottom. And although the city was not yet sacked and destroyed, its time was coming. As the prophecy foretold (Dan.

11:31; Matt. 24:15), the abomination of desolation was soon to rest upon the temple and the city. The consummation of the ancient ceremonies was at hand.

SPIRITUAL PREPARATION FOR THE FEAST

Thankfully, then, we have come far beyond these shadows of reality, having turned to the Lord Himself. And we know that "the Lord is a Spirit, and where the Spirit of the Lord is, there is liberty" (2 Cor. 3:17). Therefore, as the ears of our hearts hear the call of the priestly trumpet we do not look with our physical eyes and see an animal lamb slain, but we see the true Lamb, our Lord Jesus Christ. For as Isaiah said, He "was led as a lamb to the slaughter, and was dumb, as a lamb before her shearers" (Isa. 53:7).

We are purified by His precious blood, which cleanses us from sin. His blood does not cry out for vengeance as did the blood of Abel (Heb. 12:24). Our feet are shod with the preparation of the gospel (Eph. 6:15) and we carry the rod and staff of the Lord, our Shepherd. We are comforted, as was the one who said, "Thy rod and Thy staff they comfort me" (Ps. 23:4).

Collectively, then, as the people of God, we are completely prepared for whatever comes and do not have to worry about anything. The apostle Paul wrote, "The Lord is at hand" (Phil. 4:5). And our Savior Himself told us that He will come when He is not expected (Luke 12:40).

So, "Let us keep the feast, not with old leaven, neither with the leaven of malice and wickedness, but with the unleavened bread of sincerity and truth" (1 Cor. 5:8). "Putting off the old man and his deeds, let us put on the new man" (Eph. 4:22–24), which is created in God, in humbleness of mind and a pure conscience. Indeed, let us meditate on His law by day and by night. Also, let us rid ourselves of all hypocrisy and fraud, and free ourselves of haughtiness and deceit. Then let us take up love towards God and neighbor. Thus prepared as new creatures drinking the new wine—the Holy Spirit—we will be able to properly keep the Feast, the season of these new fruits.

THE PROPER TIME OF THE FEAST

We begin the holy fast of Easter Week on March 31, and when we add to that day the five following ones (the symbol of the creation of the world), we come to the end of the fast on Saturday, April 5. Then, when Easter Sunday comes on April 6, we begin the Feast, which lasts through all the seven weeks to the holy day of Pentecost. That day, you will recall, was to the Jews the "Feast of Weeks." On it, they granted forgiveness and settled debts, in order that it might be a day of deliverance in every respect. As for us, let us keep that Feast as a symbol of the world to come, for on it we receive a pledge that we shall have everlasting life (cf. Rom 8:23; 2 Cor 1:22).

THE BLESSINGS OF THE HEAVENLY FEAST

In that great day, we will keep a perfect feast with Christ. And we will cry out with the psalmist, "I went with them to the house of God, with the voice of joy and praise, with a multitude that kept feast day" (Ps. 42:4). Then sorrow and mourning and sighing shall flee away, and gladness and joy shall be upon our heads!

May we be worthy of all this! Let us remember the poor and not forget kindness to strangers. Above all, let us love God with all our soul, and might, and strength, and our neighbor as ourselves. Let us receive those things that the eye has not seen, nor the ear heard, and which have not entered into the heart of man (1 Cor. 2:9). For all these have been prepared by God for those who love Him, through His only Son, our Lord and Savior Jesus Christ, through whom, to the Father alone, by the Holy Spirit, be glory and dominion for ever and ever. Amen.

Salute one another with a holy kiss. All the brothers and sisters who are with me salute you.

THE SECOND LETTER

A.D. 330

WICKEDNESS AND HERESY

INTRODUCTION TO THE SECOND LETTER

Athanasius had spent the year visiting his churches. The ancient chronicle says, "In this year he went through the Thebais." In that area of the ruins of ancient Thebes, many of the old temples and tombs had been made into Christian churches and monastaries. It was probably at this time that the people of the area developed the deep love and respect for their bishop they would later display in times of persecution.

In his Easter Letter of 330, he compared the condition of the wicked and the heretics with the condition of the faithful, who will hear, "Well done, good and faithful servant; you have been faithful over a few things, I will make you ruler over many things. Enter into the joy of your master" (Matt. 25:21). The wicked and the heretics, however, earn only "grief and misery in the torments of hell."

And, oh, what a contrast there is (or should be) between the holidays of the wicked and the Christian holy days! Athanasius saw the corruption of the worldly holidays in his time and condemned it. Was it right for him to be so strong?

Consider our own era. Take New Year's Eve, for example. There is a sort of anticipation of the coming celebration that is a corrupt parallel of the Christian's anticipation of Easter. But alas! The anticipation is of a drunken, adulterous brawl. When the whole crazy thing is over, there is not the good healthy feeling of the believer who has kept the Holy Feast. No, there is pollution and guilt. Warning: Beware of the feasts of the wicked!

Let us not forget the heretics. Athanasius wrote about how they pervert the Scripture. They take the truth and twist it, he said. They devise novel interpretations of the holy writings. He was undoubtedly referring to the Arians, who took some parts of Scripture and made their own deductions from them—as if the truth had been hidden there and had only just now been discovered by them. This private interpretation is how they came up with the novel doctrine that Christ is not really quite God.

We have their counterparts in our day. There are the modern Arians, such as the Jehovah's Witnesses and the followers of Victor Paul Wierwille (The Way, International). And we must add to them the disciples of "liberal" scholars such as Adolph Harnack, F.E.D. Schleiermacher, and Rudolph Bultmann. But there is a wide proliferation of others: Sun Myung Moon's Unification Church, Christian Science, Mormonism. They all do the same thing to the Scriptures, and we can only repeat Paul's warning, quoted by Athanasius: "If anyone preaches any other gospel to you than what you have received, let him be accursed" (Gal. 1:9).

LETTER II

A.D. 330

Again, brothers and sisters, Easter is coming — and joy along with it. The Lord has brought us once again to this special season of the year, so that after we have listened to the teaching that regularly comes before it, we will be able to keep the Feast appropriately.

So, then, let us celebrate this heavenly joy, together with the saints of old who kept the same Feast. Yes, they keep the Feast with us, and they are examples to us of life in Christ. Not only were they commissioned to preach the gospel, but if we look back at their lives, we will see that they also lived it. St. Paul wrote to the Corinthians, "You, therefore, follow me" (1 Cor. 4:16). Let us follow him then, because that command has been passed down to us. The admonition originally given to the church at Corinth reaches to all Christians of all time in every place. For the apostle Paul was "a teacher of all nations in faith and truth" (1 Tim. 2:7).

As a matter of fact, we get the same sort of teaching from all the saints of old. Solomon, for example, used proverbs, saying, "Hear, my children, the instruction of a father and pay attention to get understanding, for I give you a good gift; do not forsake my word; for I was an obedient son to my father, and beloved in the sight of my mother" (Prov. 4:1).

A good father, you see, uses the right methods of instruction — and lives up to his teaching himself. That way he won't give opponents an opportunity to say, "You that teach others, why don't you teach yourself?" (Rom. 2:21). Rather, like a good servant, he behaves so that not only is he right with God, but he also has a good influence on others. Then when, as in the Lord's parable, he has doubled the grace committed to him, he will hear, "Good and faithful servant, you have been faithful in a little, I will set you over much: enter into the joy of your Lord" (Matt. 25:21).

THE WICKED'S DEGRADED CONDITION

Since we are always supposed to be doers of what the Lord tells us rather than just hearers, let us especially be doers during the days of the Feast. By thus imitating the lives of the saints, we will enter into the joy of our Lord in heaven. *That* joy is not temporary and fleeting; it stays with us.

Evildoers have deprived themselves of this joy and will suffer the consequences: grief and misery in the torments of hell. People like this cannot even be compared with the saints of God, for not only is their behavior evil, but their minds are perverted, no longer demonstrating much of the image of God. They barely measure up to the level of animals, and their uncontrolled drive for pleasure can be compared to the behavior of lustful stallions (Jer. 5:8).

Because of their trickiness, their crimes, and their horrible sins, they are called a "generation of vipers" (Luke 3:7). Having come so low as to crawl in the dirt like snakes, they think only of what they can see and feel, valuing such things above everything else. Thus they gloat over what they can experience with the five senses, looking out for their own desires instead of serving God.

Still, it was when humanity was in this state that the Word—the Son—came to seek and to find that which was lost. Even before He came, He tried to restrain us from such foolishness, crying out, "Don't be like the horse and the mule which have no understanding, and whose mouth must be held in with bit and bridle" (Ps. 32:9). And because His own people were careless and acted as the wicked did, Isaiah, praying in the Spirit, said, "You are to me like merchants of Phoenicia" (Isa. 23:2).

THE SAD EFFECTS OF NEGLECTING GOD

The avenging Spirit protests against these evil people, saying, "Lord, in Your city You will despise their image" (Ps. 73:20). They had become so foolish — they had become so lacking in understanding — that in their busy minds they compared the Divine Wisdom (the Son) to themselves, thinking they could invent something equivalent to Him. As the apostle Paul said, "professing themselves to be wise, they became fools, and changed the glory of the incorruptible God into the likeness of the corruptible image of man, and birds, and four-footed beasts, and creeping things. . . . Therefore God gave them over to a reprobate mind to do those things which are not convenient" (Rom. 1:22,23,28).

They did not listen to the prophetic voice that asked, "To what have you likened the Lord, and with what have you compared Him?" (Isa. 40:18). Nor did they listen to David, who prayed about people like them, saying, "All those that make them [idols] are like them, and all those who put their trust in them" (Ps. 115:8). They were so blind to the truth that they considered a stone to be God. Like creatures without normal eyesight, they groped about in the dark. As the prophet Isaiah cried, "They hear indeed, but they do not understand; they see indeed, but they do not perceive; for their heart has grown fat, and their ears have grown dull" (Isa. 6:9,10).

THE FEASTS OF THE WICKED

Those people who do not observe the Lord's feasts are like that even today. They invent holidays (cf. 1 Kings 12:32,33), but the result is days of sorrow rather than days of gladness. "For there is no peace to the wicked" (Isa. 48:22), as the Lord says. And as we are also told, "Gladness and joy are taken from their mouth" (Jer. 7:34). Yes, the feasts of the wicked are hollow.

CHRIST OUR EXAMPLE

But the wise servants of the Lord, who have really put on the new nature created in the likeness of God (Eph. 4:24), listen to what He says. They apply to themselves the commandment given to Timothy: "Set an example for the believers in speech, in conduct, in love, in faith, in purity" (1 Tim. 4:12). They keep the Easter Feast so properly that even unbelievers, seeing their orderliness, must say, "God is truly with them" (1 Cor. 14:25).

Just as someone who receives an apostle receives the Lord who sent him, so someone who follows the saints' example ends up following the Lord. The apostle Paul, you will remember, said, "Follow me as I follow Christ" (1 Cor. 11:1). Our prime example, of course, is our Savior. He demonstrated the fullness of His deity when He told His disciples: "Learn of Me, for I am meek and lowly in heart, and you shall find rest for your souls" (Matt. 11:29).

The same is true of the occasion on which He put water in a basin, tied a towel around His waist, and washed His disciples' feet. At that time He told them, "Understand what I have done. You call Me Master and Lord, and you tell the truth, for I am. If therefore I, your Lord and Master, have washed your feet, you also ought to wash one another's feet: for I have given you an example, that as I have done to you, you also should do" (John 13:12–15).

O, dear brothers and sisters! How can we possibly praise our Savior's lovingkindness enough? How much volume and what kind of a "trumpet" should we use to extol such help as He gives us here? Not only do we bear His image, but He gives us His life as a pattern of heavenly behavior, so that we can follow Him.

Thus, we have from Him examples so that: if we suffer, we should not threaten our oppressors; if we are abused, we should not call names back, but should bless those who curse us; and in everything we should commit ourselves to God, who judges correctly (1 Peter 2:21–23). Christians who take that attitude and live according to the Scriptures will be partakers of Christ.

They will also be imitators of apostolic behavior. As a matter of fact, if the apostle Paul were around them, he would praise them just as he did the Corinthians: "I commend you for always keeping me in mind and carrying on the tradition I handed on to you" (1 Cor. 11:2).

HERESIES ARE PERVERSIONS OF THE TRUTH

Other men came along who used Paul's words, but they wanted to "obey" them their way. So they twisted what he said to fit their schemes. They are like the followers of Hymenaeus and Alexander — and before them, the Sadducees. These people, as St. Paul said, "made shipwreck of faith" (1 Tim. 1:19), since they were confused about the mystery of the resurrection (2 Tim. 2:18).

That is undoubtedly why he made special note of the fact that the Corinthians had held fast to the traditions just as he had handed them on. Paul was emphasizing that we should hold the same views on the gospel that our teachers held. It was not only outwardly that these wicked men disguised themselves. When the Lord said they put on sheep's clothing and looked like whitewashed tombstones, He meant that they put on a very good pretense.

So these deceivers spoke the divine words, while inside they had evil intentions.

Of course, the first to do this sort of thing was the serpent, the devil, who was the inventor of wickedness in the first place. He put on a disguise to talk with Eve, and in that form he deceived her. But in his train are all these inventors of heresies, who, sure enough, refer to the Scriptures but do not believe the orthodox faith handed down to us by our Fathers. Instead, they call these truths "traditions of men." The fact is, they have gone astray because they do not really know the Scriptures — nor their power.

GOD'S DOCTRINE AND MEN'S TRADITIONS

You can see, then, that it was right for Paul to praise the Corinthians, because their views were in agreement with the traditions he had given them. Further, it was quite appropriate for the Lord to reprove the Jews when He said, "Why do you break the commandments of God on account of your traditions?" (Matt. 15:3). For they changed the commandments handed down to them from God to suit their own foolish ideas.

Instead of following God's tradition, they embraced the traditions of men.

Later, the apostle Paul instructed the Galatians, who were in danger of doing the same thing, "If anyone preaches to you anything besides what you have received, let him be accursed" (Gal. 1:9). There is no association at all between the orthodox faith and the fancies of human invention. The Fathers of the church are the ministers of truth, preaching the kingdom of heaven. But those false teachers who get carried off in the opposite direction have no real hope. All they can do is go through the motions of life, thinking that when they die they will cease to exist. So we hear them say, "Let us eat and drink, for tomorrow we die" (Isa. 22:13).

That is why the blessed Luke reproves man-made traditions and ideas, while handing down the words of the apostles. He made his purpose quite clear in the beginning of the Gospel he wrote: "Many people have written narrations of the events that happened among us, using the traditions handed down to us by the original disciples and other eyewitnesses. Since I have clung to the truth from the beginning, I decided to write it all down in order and send it to you, excellent Theophilus, so that you may know the truth about what you have been taught" (Luke 1:1–4).

What the apostles received, they passed on without change, so that the doctrine of the mysteries (the sacraments) and Christ would remain correct. The Divine Word — the Son of God — wants us to be *their* disciples. It is appropriate for them to be our teachers, and it is necessary for us to submit to their teaching alone. Only from them and those who have faithfully taught their doctrine do we get, as Paul writes, "faithful words, worthy of complete acceptance" (1 Tim. 1:15). With them we are back to ground level, because they did not become disciples as a result of what they heard from others. Rather, they were eyewitnesses and servants of God the Word, and they handed down what they heard directly from Him.

Some of them told about the great miracles performed by our Savior, and preached His eternal godhead. Others wrote about Him being born as a baby of the Virgin Mary, and announced the festival of the holy Passover, saying, "Christ our Passover is sacrificed" (1 Cor. 5:7). As a result of their testimony, each of us and all of us together, and all the churches in the world, know "that Christ rose from the dead, of the seed of David, according to the Gospel" (2 Tim. 2:8).

Let us not forget what Paul wrote to the Corinthians concerning the Lord's resurrection (cf. 1 Cor. 15:12–57). By that resurrection "He destroyed him who had the power of death; that is, the devil" (Heb. 2:14). Yes, and He raised *us* up along with Himself, because he cut loose the hold death had on us. He gave us a blessing instead of a curse, joy instead of grief, and a feast instead of mourning—the holy and joyful Feast of Easter.

Thus, with our hearts full of all that He has done for us, we rejoice continually, as Paul commanded: "Praying without ceasing, in everything giving thanks" (1 Thess. 5:17,18). So when Easter time comes around, we make it and everything connected with it known, just as we received it from the Fathers.

THE DATES OF THE EASTER SEASON

Thus we write once again. Holding to the apostolic tradition, we remember each other when we meet for prayer. We keep the Easter Feast together, giving thanks to the Lord with one voice. Having received the grace of the Lord, and being followers of the saints who went before us, "we shall make our praise in the Lord all the day" (Ps. 35:28). Properly keeping the Feast in this way, we will share in the joy of heaven.

We begin the forty-day fast on March 9. Easter Week begins on April 13. Therefore, we keep the Feast on Sunday, April 19, and follow it up with the seven weeks to Pentecost. Throughout the whole time, let us rejoice and delight in Christ Jesus our Lord, through whom to the Father be glory and dominion by the Holy Spirit, for ever and ever. Amen.

The brothers and sisters who are with me greet you. Greet one another with a holy kiss.

THE THIRD LETTER

A.D. 331

GRATITUDE AND THANKSGIVING

INTRODUCTION TO THE THIRD LETTER

During this year, Athanasius was called before Emperor Constantine to answer charges his enemies had made against him. While he was there, the time came to write the Easter Letter, and the faithful bishop found a way to send it back. He mentions his troubles at the beginning of the letter in a brief note about "those who afflict us."

His main theme this year is the distinction between thankful and unthankful people. By the skillful use of Scripture he uncovers the condition of the unthankful, pointing out that unthankfulness is wicked. Unthankfulness quenches the Spirit, so people who lack gratitude are bound to be in darkness.

Ah, but the faithful people of God are thankful. They praise the Lord. And Athanasius gives a list of Old Testament examples, before returning to his own troubles. But note that he does not use *his* difficulties as an occasion to complain. Rather, he says, the more they persecute me the more I'll praise the Lord. I will not be unthankful.

It seems that the same warning and exhortation is proper and appropriate even in our day. Isn't it true that unthankful people are sour and scheming, always trying to get what's coming to them? And do they not miss the blessing of God?

If you let your mind wander through thoughts of people you know and have known, you'll discover that it isn't always those who seem the most blessed in a worldly sense who are thankful. As a matter of fact, it often seems that the reverse is true. The poor and the afflicted praise the Lord, while the rich and the comfortable gripe and grumble and complain. The Scriptures are clear: whatever our circumstances, we are to praise the Lord.

So count your blessings, Christian! Let us be thankful unto Him! Yea, and with Moses, and Athanasius after him, "I will sing unto the Lord, for He has triumphed gloriously" (Exod. 15:1; KJV).

LETTER III
A.D. 331

Again, brothers and sisters, Easter day is coming! This day above all others should be given over to prayer and praise, as the Scriptures command. As your bishop, I dare not forget to give you a message for the season. Those who trouble us have tried to make it impossible for us to announce this season to you. Nevertheless, thanks to God, "who comforts the afflicted" (2 Cor. 7:6), we have not been silenced or overcome by the wickedness of our accusers. Rather, obeying the voice of truth, we join you in announcing the Feast.

The God of all has commanded, "Speak and the children of Israel shall keep the Passover" (Num. 9:2). And in the Psalm the Spirit exhorts, "Blow the trumpet in the new moons, in the solemn day of your feast" (Ps. 81:3). Similarly, the prophet cried, "Keep your feasts, O Judah" (Nah. 1:15). So I'm not sending this letter to you as if you did not know what is going on. I'm sending it to people who understand, so that you will be aware that although men have separated us, God has brought us back together again. We come to the same Feast together and always worship the same God.

CHRIST: OBJECT OF THE FEAST

We do not keep the Easter festival as people who are superstitious about days having power in themselves. The apostle Paul chided those who do that sort of thing when he said, "You observe days, and months, and times, and years"

(Gal. 4:10). Rather, we consider the day to be special and holy because of the Feast. With that attitude, all of us who serve the Lord everywhere will be pleasing to God. When the blessed Paul announced the nearness of this joyful time of the Christian year, he did not stress the day. Instead, he spoke of the Lord, because of whom we keep the Feast: "Christ, our Passover is sacrificed" (1 Cor. 5:7). He wanted all of us to turn our thoughts to the eternity of the Word—the Son of God—and draw near to Him. For what, after all, is the Feast, but an act of serving Him with the soul? And what is that service but extended prayer and continuous thanksgiving to God?

Unthankful people, having strayed from prayer and thanksgiving, deprive themselves of the resulting joy. For joy and gladness are truly "taken from their mouth" (Jer. 7:34). Consequently, the divine Word does not allow them to have peace, "For there is no peace to the wicked, says the Lord" (Isa. 48:22). Rather, they end up with anguish and sorrow.

That is why the one who owed ten thousand talents was not forgiven by the Lord (Matt. 18:34). Having been forgiven of a large debt, he was unkind to those who owed him small ones. In the end, he paid the penalty for both the large and the small debts. That was quite proper, because the right thing for him to have done, after having experienced kindness, would have been to be merciful to his fellow servant.

Similarly, the man who received one talent, tied it up in a napkin, and hid it in the ground was thrown out as an unthankful person. Because of his attitude he was told, "You wicked and lazy servant, you knew that I reap where I sowed not, and gathered where I have not strewn; you ought therefore to have put my money into the bank, and on my return, I should have received my own. Take therefore the talent from him, and give it to the man that has ten talents" (Matt. 25:26–28).

Since it was his duty to return to his lord what belonged to him, he should have acknowledged the kindness of the one who gave it to him—and the value of what he had received. His lord wasn't really a hard man; if he had been, he wouldn't have given it to him in the first place. Nor was that which was given something unprofitable and useless, for then there would have been no fault. No, his lord was really good, and that which was given was capable of bearing fruit.

USE PROFITABLY THE GRACE OF GOD

There is a proverb that says, "He who withholds corn in seed-time is cursed" (Prov. 11:26). In the same way, someone who is careless about grace and hides it without allowing it to work in him is appropriately thrown out as a wicked and thankless person. On the other hand, those who increase their talents are praised: "Well done, good and faithful servant, you have been faithful in a little, I will place you over much; enter into the joy of your Lord" (Matt. 25:23).

Now, dear brothers and sisters, our will to do should keep pace with the grace of God. For if our will sits idly by, neglecting His grace, the enemy will discover our emptiness and move in on us. That was what happened to the one from whom the demon went out: "for having gone through dry places, he took seven other spirits more wicked than himself; and returning and finding the house empty, he dwelt there, and the last state of that man was worse than the first" (Matt. 12:43–45). Why? Because turning away from virtue makes room for unclean spirits.

In addition, we have an apostolic injunction that the grace given to us should not be unprofitable. The things St. Paul wrote to his disciples personally, he lays on us through them, as for example, "Neglect not the gift that is in you" (1 Tim. 4:14). And there is a proverb to the same effect: "He who tills his land shall be satisfied with bread, but the paths of the lazy man are strewn with thorns" (Prov. 12:11; cf. 15:19).

Further, the Holy Spirit warns us not to fall into such things, saying, "Break up your fallow ground, do not sow among thorns" (Jer. 4:3). The reason is that when someone thinks so little of the grace God has given him that he neglects it, he is headed for trouble. Without doubt he will soon be all wrapped up in the cares of life, and shortly he will be living just for the pleasures of the flesh. Then when persecution comes, he rejects the faith and his life is barren.

SPIRITUAL ZEAL COMPARED WITH FIRE

As Jeremiah pointed out, such negligence is dangerous: "Cursed is he who is careless in the work of the Lord" (Jer. 48:10). Anyone who enlists in the service of the Lord should be diligent and attentive. Then when he has wiped sin out of his life by his zeal, he will be prepared to draw near to God—who the Scripture calls a consuming fire (Deut. 4:24; 9:3; Heb. 12:29).

We must remember that God, "Who makes His angels spirits," is Himself a spirit, and He makes "flames of fire His servants" (Ps. 104:4). Thus, when Israel had left Egypt, He forbade the people to even touch the mountain where He was giving the Law, because they were far from being "on fire" for the Lord. He did, however, call the blessed Moses to that mountain. Moses was totally committed to Him and clung to His grace, so God said, "Let Moses alone draw near" (Exod. 24:2). So Moses climbed up the mountain into the cloud, and although that mountain smoked with the heat and presence of the Lord, Moses was unharmed. Rather, through "the words of the Lord which are pure silver refined in a furnace" (Ps. 12:6), he came down more pure than when he went up.

QUENCHING THE HOLY SPIRIT

We can thus see why Paul, not wanting the grace of the Spirit given to us to grow cold, exhorts us, "Quench not the Spirit" (1 Thess. 5:19). The only way we can continue to be partakers of Christ is to cling until the end to the Holy Spirit, who was given to us at the beginning (Matt. 10:22; Heb. 3:6). Paul said, "Quench not" not because the Spirit is under the power of men, but because evil and unthankful men certainly *do wish* to quench the Spirit. Demonstrating their impurity, they drive the Spirit away by their unholy deeds. "For the holy Spirit of admonition flees from guile, and dwells not in a body under the influence of sin; but departs from foolish thoughts."[1] But people

[1]Wisdom 1:4,5.

like this are foolish and deceitful and love sin. They still walk as if they were in darkness, not having that "Light which lights every man who comes into the world" (John 1:9).

We are told that the word of the Lord was in Jeremiah like a burning fire. His response was, "Holding it back makes me very weary, I can no longer endure it" (Jer. 20:9). Our Lord Jesus Christ, being so good and loving humanity so much, came in the flesh to bring this kind of fire to the earth. "Oh! that it were already kindled!" He said (Luke 12:49). He wanted people to repent rather than to die (as we find in Ezekiel). Therefore, He wished to have the evil and the wickedness burned out of men so that, being purified, they would be fruitful (Ezek. 18:23,32). We know that the Word He sows will be productive—some thirty-, some sixty-, and some a hundredfold (Mark 4:20).

THE INGRATITUDE OF THE WICKED

As an example, consider Cleopas and his companion on the road to Emmaus (Luke 24). At first their faith was weak from lack of knowledge, but the words of our Savior fired them up and brought forth the fruits of knowing Him. And St. Paul, when caught by this fire of God, did not run around telling people about it. Nevertheless, after he had experienced God's grace he became a preacher of the Word.

On the other hand, we have nine lepers whom the Lord cleansed from their leprosy, yet who were not thankful to Him (Luke 17). They certainly were not like Paul! Judas, who had the privilege of being an apostle, was not called a disciple of the Lord. On the contrary, at the very end, while eating bread with our Savior, he "lifted up his heel against Him," and became a traitor (John 13:18).

People like that will get what they deserve for their foolishness. Because of their lack of gratitude, their hope will be futile, for there is no hope for the ungrateful. The final fire, prepared for the devil and his angels, awaits those who disregard divine light. And the unthankful belong in that category.

But the faithful and true servants of the Lord are very different. Knowing that the Lord loves thankful people, they never cease to praise Him, and they regularly thank Him. In both good times and bad times they offer praise and thanksgiving to God. They worship the Lord, the God of times, without regard to what the times are like.

A good example from ancient days is Job, who thought about these things when he prospered. Then when troubles came, he patiently endured; when he suffered, he gave thanks. Or consider David, who sang praises in a time of great difficulty, saying, "I will bless the Lord at all times" (Ps. 34:1). Or St. Paul, who thanked God in every one of his letters. First of all, he didn't turn away from God in good times. But he also was happy to face problems, knowing that "trouble develops endurance and endurance builds strong character, which in turn strengthens our hope and hope is no mockery" (Rom. 5:3–5).

PRAISE AND THANKSGIVING IN TIMES OF TROUBLE

With such men as these going before us as examples, let *us* give thanksgiving in all kinds of times. But right now especially, when we have tremendous tribulations and the heretics are inciting people against us, we will praise the Lord.[2] Yes, we will use the words of the ancient saints, "All these things have come upon us, yet we have not forgotten You" (Ps. 44:17). In those days the Jews were attacked by the Edomites and were oppressed by other enemies of Jerusalem. Nevertheless, they did not give themselves up for lost. Instead, they sang more praises to the Lord.

All right then, brothers and sisters, if they interfere with our speaking of the word of the Lord, we will proclaim it all the more. And if we are persecuted we will sing Psalms, because God counts us worthy to be despised and to work eagerly for the truth. Yes, the more we are harrassed, the more we will give thanks!

The apostle Paul, who thanked God all the time, urges us to

[2]Remember that this letter was written at a time when Athanasius had been called before the emperor to answer false charges made by the Arian heretics.

approach God in the same manner, "Let your requests, with thanksgiving, be made known to God" (Phil. 4:6). And wanting us to continue in that, he says, "At all times give thanks; pray without ceasing" (1 Thess. 5:17). He knew that believers are strong when engaged in thanksgiving. He also knew that when we rejoice we go right over the enemy's walls, like the saints who sang, "By your strength I can attack any enemy, go over any wall" (Ps. 18:29).

So then, let us stand firm all the time, but especially right now even though we have many troubles and many heretics are violently attacking us. Let us, dear brothers and sisters, celebrate with thanksgiving the holy Easter Feast coming up. Further, let us gird up our minds (1 Peter 1:13), like Jesus Christ our Savior, of whom it is written, "Righteousness shall be the belt of His loins, and faithfulness shall gird His body" (Isa. 11:5). Each of us is to have in his hand the staff that came out of the root of Jesse (Isa. 11:1), and our feet are to be shod with the preparation of the gospel (Eph. 6:15).

Therefore, being so well prepared, let us keep the Feast as Paul tells us to keep it, "Not with the old leaven, but with the unleavened bread of sincerity and truth" (1 Cor. 5:7). That way we will reverently think of Christ and keep our faith in Him, and we will not dirty ourselves by getting mixed up with heretics and strangers to the truth—whose behavior and desires will destroy them. No, rejoicing in all our troubles, we break through the iron furnace of slavery to sin (Deut. 4:20) and cross over the terrible Red Sea to salvation (cf. Ps. 106:9).

And therefore when we see the confusion of the heretics, we will join Moses in that great song of praise, "We will sing unto the Lord, for He has triumphed gloriously" (Exod. 15:1). Then, singing praises and seeing the doom of sinners who have come against us, we will go on with the Lord.

Finally, purifying our hearts with the fast of forty days — along with prayers, discipline, and good works — we shall be ready to eat the holy Passover in the heavenly Jerusalem.

THE DATES OF THE EASTER SEASON

The beginning of the fast of forty days is March 1. Then, after we have been purified and prepared by those days, we will begin the Holy Week of Easter on Monday, April 5. During that week we should continue to watch and pray and fast, preparing ourselves for that "anointing of our doorposts with precious blood, by which we escape the destroyer" (cf. Exod. 12:7,23). Our fast will cease on Saturday evening, April 10, for on that night we hear the angels say, "Why do you seek the living among the dead? He has risen!" (Luke 24:5). Next day is the first day of the great week — April 11, the day on which the Lord rose and gave us peace toward our neighbors.

After we have kept the Easter Feast according to His will, let us keep an attitude of expectation through the seven weeks till Pentecost, the day of the gift of the Holy Spirit. Then indeed, we shall give thanks to the Lord at all times, through whom to the Father be glory and dominion, by the Holy Spirit, forever and ever. Amen.

Greet one another with a holy kiss. The brothers and sisters who are with me greet you. I pray, dear ones, whom I long to see, that you may be healthy and that you may remember us in the Lord.

THE FOURTH LETTER

A.D. 332

PASSOVER FULFILLED IN CHRIST THE LAMB

INTRODUCTION TO THE FOURTH LETTER

As the year 332 began, St. Athanasius was still in Constantinople, answering the accusations of his enemies. They were refuted, and Emperor Constantine highly approved of the young bishop.

Athanasius' trip home was delayed by a number of things, including a long illness. The Easter Letter was sent on ahead of him, and he returned to Alexandria midway through the fast. At the end of the letter, Athanasius notes that he has put the letter in the hands of Ablavius, prefect of the Praetorium, who sent it to Alexandria by a soldier. Ablavius was a great favorite of Constantine, serving him well and, Athanasius says, "fears God in truth."

The message this year is that the Christian festival of the Resurrection celebrates the grand and complete fulfillment of all that was pictured in the ancient Feast of the Passover. Sin, death, and the devil are defeated, and we, putting on Christ, celebrate the Feast. No longer do we need to go to a certain city, such as Jerusalem; the celebration is commanded for every church everywhere.

In the Scriptures, Christ is recognized as the true and final Passover Lamb. Athanasius recognized that fact, and so do we today. It is still true and will always be. So this year, when you gather with the brothers and sisters for the Great Eucharist, hear the Savior say, "Take, eat and drink; this is My body and blood."

LETTER IV

A.D. 332

I know this letter is late, dear brothers and sisters. Still, I hope you will forgive the delay, which came about because I am traveling so far from home and because I have had a long illness. Since these two problems hindered my reply and since there have been some unusually severe storms, this letter will be quite late. However, in spite of the distance and my distressing illness, I have not forgotten you. Herein, then, as is my duty, I announce to you the Easter Feast.

Although this letter is much later than the usual announcement, it should not be considered ill-timed. Our enemies have been put to shame and reproved by the church because they persecuted us for no good reason. Therefore, we may now sing a festal song of praise, such as the triumphant hymn Israel sang against Pharaoh, "We will sing unto the Lord, for he has triumphed gloriously; the horse and rider he has thrown into the sea" (Exod. 15:1). Thus, we appropriately proceed as usual: from feast to feast. Once again holy self-examination stirs up our minds and keeps our consciences on guard to think on good things.

FEASTS ESTABLISHED ON SPECIAL OCCASIONS

We do not act like mourners during these days. Rather, we put down the appetites of our bodies in order to refresh ourselves with spiritual food. In this way we gain strength to conquer our enemies (as, for example, Judith did when she fasted and prayed before killing Holofernes and overcoming the enemies of Israel[1]). When the whole nation of Israel was about to perish, blessed Esther defeated the tyrant's anger simply by fasting and praying to God. By faith she changed the ruin of her people into safety (Esther 4:16)! Those days are feast days for Israel (Esther 9:20–28);[2] they used to call a feast when an enemy was slain or a conspiracy against the people was broken up, and Israel was delivered. That is why Moses established the Feast of the Passover — because Pharaoh was killed and the people were delivered from bondage.

So then, especially when tyrants were slain, temporal feasts and holidays were established in Judea. Now, however, the devil, that tyrant against the whole world, is slain. Therefore, our Feast does not relate only to time, but to eternity. It is a heavenly Feast! We do not announce it as a shadow or a picture or a type, but as the real thing.

THE GLORIOUS CHRISTIAN FESTIVAL

Israel ate the meat of a dumb lamb to complete the Passover, and having done so, they smeared their doorposts with blood and laughed at the destroyer. But we eat of the Word of the Father, the Son our Savior. We have the lintels of our hearts sealed with the blood of the New Covenant (Matt. 26:28). Therefore we acknowledge the grace given to us by our Savior, who said, "Behold I have given you authority to tread upon serpents and scorpions, and over all the power of the enemy" (Luke 10:19).

Death does not reign anymore! Instead of death there is life, since our Lord said, "I am the life" (John 14:6). For His people everything is filled with gladness and rejoicing, as the Psalm says, "The Lord reigns, let the earth rejoice" (Ps. 97:1). For when death reigned, "sitting down by the rivers of Babylon, we wept" (Ps. 137:1) and mourned because we were experiencing

[1]Judith 13:8.
[2]Judith 9.

the bitterness of captivity. But now that death and the kingdom of the devil is abolished, we are filled with joy and gladness. God is no longer known only in Judea, but in all the earth. "Their voice has gone forth, and the knowledge of Him has filled the whole earth" (Ps. 76:1; 19:4).

What follows, dear brothers and sisters, is obvious. We do not come to such a feast with dirty clothes, but with our consciences clothed, so to speak, with pure garments. We need to put on our Lord Jesus, so that we can celebrate the Feast with Him. We demonstrate that we are clothed with Him when:

—we love virtue;
—we are enemies of wickedness;
—we actively engage in temperance;
—we put to death erotic fantasies and attitudes;
—we love righteousness rather than wickedness;
—we aim to live without undue luxury;
—we have strength of mind;
—we do not forget the poor, but open our doors to all;
—we assist humility, but hate pride.

It was by these things that ancient Israel, after having fought the battle that pictured what was to come, came to the Feast. All that we would do and receive was foreshadowed in God's dealings with them.

PICTURES AND SHADOWS ARE NOW REALITY

Now the pictures and shadows and types have all been fulfilled and accomplished. So we, dear brothers and sisters, should no longer consider the Feast a figurative one. We do not go up to the earthly city of Jerusalem to sacrifice the Passover. That ancient Jewish practice is no longer suitable. If we followed their practice, we would be celebrating the Easter season inappropriately. No, in accordance with the directions of the apostles, let us go beyond the pictures and types and sing the new song of praise. They, being in the presence of the Truth, asked our Savior, "Where do you want us to make the Passover ready for You?" (Matt. 26:17).

No longer was the old Passover ceremony—belonging to the earthly Jerusalem—to be held. Nor was the New Feast[3] to be celebrated only there, but rather wherever God wished it to be held. And now He wished it to be celebrated everywhere, so that "in every place incense and a sacrifice might be offered to Him" (Mal. 1:11).

In the historical account, Israel was commanded to keep the Feast of the Passover in Jerusalem and nowhere else. Nevertheless, everything pertaining to those times was finally fulfilled. When that had happened and the time had come for the gospel to be preached everywhere, the disciples, in preparation for spreading the Feast everywhere, asked our Savior that significant question, "Where do you want us to make ready?" Since our Savior was making the change from the type or shadow to the spiritual reality, He gave them the New Covenant promise. That is, He promised them that they would not eat the flesh of a lamb anymore, *but His own*: "Take, eat and drink; this is My body and My blood" (cf. Matt. 26:26–28).

Well, dear friends, when we are nourished by His body and blood, we *properly* keep the Feast of the Passover.

THE TIME FOR OBSERVING EASTER

We begin the fast of Easter Week on March 27 and end it on Saturday, April 1. Then we celebrate the Feast on Sunday, April 2. Afterward come the holy days of Pentecost, days which show forth the world to come. For in eternity we will be with Christ forever, praising God Almighty in Christ Jesus. Through Him, with all the saints, we say to the Lord, Amen.

Greet one another with a holy kiss. All the brothers and sisters who are with me greet you.

We have sent this letter from the emperor's court through an attendant officer, to whom it was given by Ablavius, the prefect of the Praetorium, who truly fears God. I am still at the court, having been summoned by the emperor Constantine to see

[3]Easter, the Feast of the Resurrection.

him. Some Meletians[4] who were present sought out of envy to influence the emperor against us. Their charges, however, were easily proven false, and they were driven away in shame as liars. Their names, by the way, were Callinicus, Ision, Eudaemon, and Geloeus[5] Hieracammon, who because of the shame of his name calls himself Eulozius.

[4]The Meletians, remember, were a group that had split away from the church.
[5]The name means "laughable."

THE FIFTH LETTER

A.D. 333

CHRIST SATISFIES COMPLETELY: RESPOND ACCORDINGLY

INTRODUCTION TO THE FIFTH LETTER

Although his enemies (enemies also of God) were at this time thinking up new charges to present to the emperor, St. Athanasius carried on his ministry to the flock. Again he visited the churches, giving personal attention to needs and problems and serving the poor and needy. Intensely devoted to the Lord, he followed the annual liturgical cycle from feast to feast, prayer to prayer, fast to fast, advancing from one holy day to the next with intense zeal.

Anticipating the Easter Feast, Athanasius turns his thoughts this year to the fact that at the Table we eat the food of life and drink from the life-giving fountain of the Savior's precious blood.

In thinking of this, he naturally considers what we can do in return; after all, we owe everything. Nevertheless, there is no adequate return for what the Lord has given us. We do offer Him a holy life, but even that is supplied to us by Him.Thus we must properly acknowledge — by praise, thanksgiving, and a holy life—His gifts to us.

What a contrast the heathen, the Jews, the schismatics, and the heretics offer! Blinded by sin and doing what they *think* is right rather than following the Lord's instructions, they utterly fail to receive what He offers. That tragedy will not, however, befall those who eat the Passover in truth and sincerity. Says Athanasius, "For the Passover truly is a turning from wickedness to godliness, and a conversion from death to life."

Who in all the world is satisfied today? Just as always it is those who eat His body and drink His blood, those who eat the Lord's Passover, who rejoice in having all their needs fulfilled.

Owing Him everything, we want to give a proper gift. What acceptable offering can we give to the High King of Heaven? Alas, we seem so poor. Yet by our union with Him, He gives us all we need. We can say with Paul, "I have been crucified with Christ; it is no longer I who live, but Christ lives in me" (Gal. 2:20).

LETTER V

A.D. 333

We follow the clock and the calendar around, brothers and sisters, from prayer-time to prayer-time, from feast to feast. More than that, we advance year to year, from this year's fast to next year's, from this year's holiday to next year's holiday. So as the year has moved around, the time has come once again for a new beginning—this year's announcement of the blessed Passover, the date on which our Lord was sacrificed.

Because He was so sacrificed, we eat, as it were, the Lord of Life. And, being people who are always thirsty, we drink continuously and happily of His precious blood, as from a fountain. For we really are always thirsty, and He is always prepared to satisfy that thirst. As He, in His love, said on the day of a certain feast, "If anyone is thirsty, let him come to me and drink" (John 7:37).

But the grace of the true Feast, the Great Feast, is not just available at one time and never again. *That* grace is always present. *Whenever* anyone seeks the Savior, He is available.

Nor does the splendid brilliance of His grace ever suffer an eclipse. No, it is always at hand to enlighten the inner thoughts of those who really want it. Great good comes to people who, enlightened by the grace of God, make it their habit to apply the truths of Holy Scripture to their lives. They receive just such a blessing as the psalmist describes: "Blessed is the man who has not walked in the counsel of the ungodly, nor stood in the way of sinners, nor sat in the seat of corrupters. But his delight is in the law of the Lord, and He meditates in His law day and night" (Ps. 1:1,2).

Those blessings come because the person who accepts God's grace is not illumined by mere physical light from the sun, the moon, or even the whole host of stars. Rather, he glows all over with the radiant brilliance of God.

ALL CHRISTIANS UNITE IN THE FEAST

Remember, dear friends, that we are given this annual celebration of the Easter Feast by the God who established it in the first place. It was God the Father who sent His Son to be slain for our salvation, and thus gave us a reason for the Holy Feast. Every year the Feast, coming as it does at the same time, is a witness to that great act of the Father, Son, and Holy Spirit.

And so, knowing of the death of Christ on the cross, we proceed from the daily routine of life in this world to the Feast, and in that celebration God gives us the joy of His glorious salvation. For every year He brings us all together and unites us all in spirit, although we meet in many different places. We share everywhere the same prayers and the same grace in our common Feast.

HUMAN NATURE INADEQUATE TO REPAY GOD

Well then, brothers and sisters, why don't we acknowledge His grace in a way proper to this great holy day, this blessed Feast? Why don't we repay our Benefactor? Of course it is impossible to adequately repay God. Still, it is really wicked for people who have received such a gracious gift not even to acknowledge it. Nature itself is enough to show that we are unable to pay the debt, but even our own desires rebuke our unthankfulness.

St. Paul, expressing reverence for the greatness of God's gift, said, "And who is sufficient for these things?" (2 Cor. 2:16). For the Father freed the world by the blood of our Savior. And above all else, He opened the gates of heaven so the Savior would have a clear and open passage for all He brings in.

That is why one of the ancient saints, acknowledging God's grace and his own inability to repay it, said, "What shall I pay the Lord for all He has done for me?" (Ps. 116:12). He knew that instead of the death he deserved, he had been given life. He had been given freedom to replace his old slavery to sin. And he had received the kingdom of heaven instead of the grave and hell.

As we know, in the old days, "Death reigned from Adam to Moses" (Rom. 5:14). On the other hand, we have heard the voice of our Lord say, "Today you shall be with Me in Paradise" (Luke 23:43). That is why we find the ancient saints saying, "Unless the Lord had helped me, my soul would have dwelt in hell" (Ps. 94:17). Acknowledging the gift and his own inability to pay for it, the psalmist wrote, "I will take the cup of salvation and call on the name of the Lord . . . precious in His sight is the death of His saints" (Ps. 116:13,15).

With regard to His cup, our Lord said, "Are you able to drink of that cup which I am about to drink of?" (Matt. 20:22). And when His disciples indicated that they thought they were, He added, "You shall indeed drink of My cup; but as to whether you should sit on My right hand and on My left, that is not Mine to give; but to those for whom it is prepared" (Matt. 20:23).

So, my dear friends, let us be aware of the gift He has given us, even though we are unable to repay it. As far as we are able, however, let us rise to the occasion. Of course, human nature does not have the capacity to repay the Word (Christ) for such a great gift as salvation. Still, we can thank Him, even while we stand in reverent awe of Him.

In fact, how can we be more reverent than by acknowledging that God, loving humanity so much, has given such wonderful gifts to us? If we do, we shall certainly be obedient to His law and keep His commandments, and we will not be thought of as unthankful lawbreakers, doing things that ought to be despised. Remember, the Lord loves the thankful.

There is, therefore, nothing more appropriate for us to do than to offer ourselves to the Lord as did the saints of old. Let us dedicate ourselves to living not to ourselves but to the Lord, who died for us. St. Paul said, "I am crucified with Christ, but I am alive; yet not I, but Christ lives in me" (Gal. 2:20).

PROPERLY ACKNOWLEDGING GOD'S GIFTS

Consequently, dear friends in the faith, our life consists in putting the things of our Savior above the desires of our bodies. That is why the present holy season requires that we not only say such words, but that we also imitate the deeds of the godly believers who have gone before us. We imitate them when we confess Him who died; when we no longer live for ourselves but have Christ living in us; when we repay the Lord to the best of our ability — that is, not by giving anything of our own, but by returning what we have received from Him.

It is a special matter of His grace that what He asks from us is what He has given us. For He tells us, "My offerings are My own gifts" (cf. Num. 28:2, Septuagint). In other words, those things which we give Him are ours, received from Him, but they are gifts of God. Well, then, let us offer to the Lord virtuous lives and the true holiness He calls for. Yes, with all devotion and reverence let us keep the Feast to Him with those things He has sanctified for us.

THE JEWS AND THE SCHISMATICS REPROVED

As we then begin the holy pre-Easter fasts, let us treat them as having been prescribed to us by Him as a means of focusing our attention on God. We must not take the attitude held by the heathen, or the ignorant Jews, or the present-day heretics and schismatics. The heathen think the Feast is accomplished by having a big meal with an enormous abundance of food. The Jews, being mistaken about the fulfillment of the type and shadow of the Feast, still think of it in terms of the days in which it was first given. And the schismatics keep it in places apart from the church, with wild ideas about the meaning.

So, brothers and sisters, let us be superior to the heathen, keeping the Feast with sincerity of soul and purity of body. Let us also do better than the Jews, by recognizing far more than shadow and type in the Feast. Oh yes, for we are people on whom the light of truth shines and who look to the Sun of Righteousness (Mal. 4:2). Further, let us do better than the schismatics and refuse to divide the church of Christ. Let us rather eat the Passover of the Lord in one house, the catholic church.[1] For the Lord of the Passover, who gave us His holy laws, guided us to the practice of righteousness and promised the Feast (Exod. 12:46).

ALWAYS REMEMBER GOD'S KIND ACTS

The Passover truly is a turning from wickedness to godliness and a conversion from death to life. Israel was most eager to escape from Egypt and move on to Jerusalem, and today we are eager to escape death and move on to life. At the same time, Israel escaped the rule of Pharaoh and came under the leadership of Moses. Similarly, we rise up from the rule of the devil to the reign of the Savior.

Further, just as in those days there was a representation of their deliverance celebrated every year as a witness, we have one too. Remembering our salvation, we fast, meditating on death, so that we may be able to live. And we keep watch through the night, not in the way that mourners do, but as waiting for the Lord to "return from the wedding" (cf. Luke 12:36). We are even prepared to compete with each other in announcing His triumph, His victory over death.

O dear friends, how I wish that at all times we remembered and lived so as never to forget the gracious acts of God—and so as never to cease living holy lives! As the apostle Paul exhorts, "Remember Jesus Christ, that He rose from the dead" (2 Tim. 2:8). He did not say there was a limited season of remembrance. No, he wanted the Lord in our thoughts at all times. Still, because of general laziness, we put it off from day to day. Well, let's begin now. After all, that is why a particular time of

[1]In Athanasius' day, there was no *Roman* Catholic Church — and no Greek Orthodox, no American Lutheran Church, no Southern Baptist Church. All was the catholic (universal) church. May it be so again!

remembrance is established: to remind the saints of the reward of their calling and to reprove and exhort the careless.

Therefore, let us apply ourselves to righteous living between now and the Feast day, repenting of our neglect to do what we should. For none of us is free from defilement — even those who have lived on the earth for just one hour, as faithful Job tells us (Job 14:4, Septuagint). But "stretching forth to those things which are to come" (Phil. 3:13), let us pray that we will not eat the Passover unworthily and expose ourselves to danger. For the Passover is heavenly food for those who keep the Feast with pure hearts. But to those who observe it profanely and contemptuously, it brings harm and loss. The Scriptures warn, "Whoever eats and drinks unworthily is guilty of the death of the Lord" (1 Cor. 11:27).

Let us, then, not just go through the motions of the Feast, but rather prepare to approach the divine Lamb, to eat heavenly food. Let us cleanse our hands and purify our bodies. Let us keep our minds free from deceit, and let us not give ourselves up to intemperateness and the indulgence of the desires of the body. Rather, let us wholeheartedly occupy ourselves with our Lord and with holy doctrine. Then, purified and ready, we will be able to partake of the Word—Christ the Son of God (2 Peter 1:4).

THE DATES OF EASTER

We begin the holy pre-Easter fast on Monday, April 9, and end it on Saturday, April 14, for April 15 is Easter Sunday, the day of resurrection. Then, to that great Feast day, we add the seven weeks until Pentecost Sunday. That whole holy period we will celebrate with prayers, giving to our neighbors, love toward one another, and above all, a peaceable attitude. Then we shall indeed be heirs of the kingdom of heaven, through our Lord Jesus Christ, through whom to the Father be glory and dominion forever and ever. Amen.

All the brothers and sisters who are with me greet you. Greet one another with a holy kiss.

THE SIXTH LETTER

A.D. 334

GLORIFY GOD WITH YOUR BODY

INTRODUCTION TO THE SIXTH LETTER

According to the ancient chronicle, Athanasius visited the "lower country" this year. Meanwhile, his enemies had gotten together what seemed to be a solid set of charges (all false), and had him summoned to a council to be held at Caesarea under Eusebius. "No," he replied, "I'm not going there to be judged by people who are biased against me." Thus, the bishop was still home to send this year's letter.

Athanasius again touches on praise and thanksgiving; he never loses that theme. But he also dwells at some length on what the death of Christ means to us. In all the activities of the season, we must not forget that "the Lord was sacrificed that by His blood He might abolish death." He points out that Israel, having refused Him, has grief instead of gladness in its attempt to celebrate the Passover.

He also builds a strong illustration from the example of Abraham's sacrifice of Isaac, pointing out that if God had allowed that sacrifice to be completed, the Jews would have applied all the prophecies about the Savior to Isaac. That would not do, of course, for it is only He who is both God and man who could, by His stripes, heal us all.

Thus, the letter builds to its climax: Let us keep the festival in purity and joy, for the church in heaven keeps it with us. Athanasius gives us the examples of Moses, David, and Daniel, as well as the exhortation of Paul.

We modern people have an aversion to making long preparations of ourselves for any worship of God. We hope (although we know better) that a brief silent prayer puts us in a receptive frame and "pacifies" God as we move from the world to the heavenlies.

To Athanasius, this time of fasting and anticipation was a time of loving preparation: preparation of the whole being — mind, will, body, soul, and spirit — for the joyous experience of the resurrection festival. Abstention from food went with watching and prayer, holiness of thought and life, giving to the poor, and longing for the resurrection day.

We need that. Our age is one of mental and emotional religion, and we need to return to the experience of religion in which our eyes, stomachs, and fingers do holy things. Yes, our stomachs must experience the pain of preparation for the festival; our hands must consciously behave in a holy and preparatory way. Then we too shall go up to Jerusalem and eat the Passover.

Teach us what Thy love has borne,
That with loving sorrow torn
Truly contrite we may mourn:
We beseech Thee, hear us.

Gifts of light and grace bestow,
Help us to resist the foe,
Fearing what alone is woe:
We beseech Thee, hear us.

Let not sin within us reign,
May we gladly suffer pain,
If it purge away our stain:
We beseech Thee, hear us.

May we to all evil die,
Fleshly longings crucify,
Fix our hearts and thoughts on high:
We beseech Thee, hear us.[1]

—T.B. Pollock

[1]*The Hymnal* (Boston: Stanhope Press, 1924), p. 149.

LETTER VI

A.D. 334

Once again, dear friends, God has brought us to the Easter season; by His loving kindness we are once more about to assemble for it. The same God who brought Israel out of Egypt now calls us to the Feast, saying through Moses, "Take note of the month of new fruits, and keep the Passover to the Lord your God" (Deut. 16:1). And through the prophet He calls, "Keep your feasts, O Judah; pay your vows to the Lord" (Nahum 1:15). So if God Himself loves the Feast and calls us to it, it is not right, brothers and sisters, to postpone it or to observe it carelessly. We should come to it eagerly and zealously, so that with a joyful beginning here we will experience a foretaste of the heavenly Feast that is to come.

THE "PASSOVER OF THE JEWS"

If we diligently keep the Feast that is celebrated on earth, we will without doubt receive the perfect joy of heaven. As the Lord says, "I have greatly desired to eat this Passover with you before my suffering begins. For I assure you that I will not eat it again till it has been fulfilled with you in the Kingdom of God" (Luke 22:15,16). We eat the Passover when we (1) put our minds on what it is all about, (2) acknowledge the Deliverer, and (3) respond to His grace. As Paul said, "so that we may keep the feast, not with old leaven, neither with the leaven of wickedness; but with the unleavened bread of sincerity and truth" (1 Cor. 5:8).

The Lord died so that we could be freed from doing those things that lead to death. He gave His life so that our own might be rescued from the devil's traps. And what is most wonderful of all, the Word became incarnate so that we could avoid being controlled by sin, but would be able to worship God, who is a spirit, in the spirit. (Rom. 8:9–13).

A person who doesn't keep the Feast this way rejects God's grace like an unthankful person, even though he goes through the motions. Even though he believes these days are more important than others, he does not pray to the Lord who redeemed him during these same days so long ago. Even though he thinks he is keeping the Feast, the voice of the apostle Paul is meant for him in reproof, "You observe days and months and times and years: I fear that I have labored among you in vain" (Gal. 4:10,11).

We do not observe the Feast because of the *days*; we observe it because *in those days* the Lord suffered in place of us. As Paul put it, "our Passover, Christ, is sacrificed" (1 Cor. 5:7). In the same way Moses taught Israel not to think of the Feast in terms of the day, but of the Lord, saying, "It is the Lord's Passover" (Exod. 12:11).

In the Lord's time the Jews, even though they thought they celebrated the Passover, did so in vain, because they persecuted the Lord. By their own testimony it no longer bore the name of the Lord. It was not called the Passover of the Lord, but the Passover of the Jews (John 6:4). Brothers and sisters, the Passover was named after the Jews because they denied the Lord of the Passover. That is why the Lord, turning His face away from their teaching, says, "My soul hates your new moons and your sabbaths" (Isa. 1:14).

PRAISE AND THANKSGIVING

So today, the Lord rebukes those who keep the Passover the way the Jews did, just as He rebuked certain lepers whom He had cleansed. You recall that He loved the one who was thankful but was angry with the ungrateful ones, because they did not acknowledge their Deliverer. They thought more highly of their cure from leprosy than of Him who had healed them. "But one of them when he saw that he was healed, turned back, and with a loud voice glorified God, and fell on his face at the feet of Jesus giving Him thanks. He was a Samaritan. And Jesus asked, 'Did I not heal ten? What happened to the other nine? Is this stranger the only one who returned to glorify God?' " (Luke 17:15–18). Actually, this one was given much more than all the rest, for besides being healed of his leprosy he was told by the Lord, "Stand up and go on your way. Your faith has saved you" (Luke 17:19).

You see, those who give thanks and those who glorify have the same kind of feelings — they bless their Helper for the benefits they have received. That is why Paul urged everybody to "Glorify God with your body" (1 Cor. 6:20). And Isaiah commanded, "Give glory to God" (Isa. 42:12).

Caiaphas testified against our Redeemer, and the Jews treated our Lord with contempt (Matt. 26:65–68). Pilate condemned Him. But there was great exaltation and much power in the words the Father spoke to the Son, "I have glorified and will glorify again" (John 12:28). All those things He suffered for us are over and done with, but all those that concern Him as our Savior remain forever (Phil. 2:7–11).

So, brothers and sisters, let us remember these things and not be preoccupied with food, but with praising the Lord. Let us become fools for Him who died for us. As Paul said, "If we are foolish, it is for God; if we are sober-minded, it is for you; for One died for all of us, therefore, we have all died. For He died for all so that we who live should no longer live for ourselves, but for Him who died for us and rose again" (2 Cor. 5:13–15).

THE BENEFITS OF CHRIST'S DEATH

Accordingly, we ought not to live for ourselves anymore but as servants of the Lord. His grace should not be ignored, because this is a very favorable time: the day of salvation has dawned, for our Redeemer has died (2 Cor. 6:1,2). For our sakes the immortal, indestructable Word came down and took on mortal humanity for the salvation of all. Paul plainly expressed his confidence about this by saying, "Our mortal bodies shall be changed into immortal ones" (1 Cor. 15:53).

The Lord was sacrificed so that by the shedding of His blood He might abolish death. In one place He reproached those who would try unsuccessfully to receive the benefits of the shedding of His blood, because they would not appreciate the value of feeding on the flesh of the Word (Christ, the Son). He said, "What profit is there in my blood, that I go down to death?" (Ps. 30:9). But this does not mean that the Lord's descent to earth was useless, for it gained the whole world! Rather, He meant that even after His coming in the flesh, sinners would rather be without His flesh than profit by it.

You see, He took pleasure in our salvation and thought of it as a distinctive victory for Himself. On the other hand, He considered our destruction a sad loss. As to those who reject the benefits of His incarnation, one of His parables in the Gospels applies. He praised those who doubled the grace He gave, both the one who made ten talents from five and the one who made four talents from two. Both of them had done the right thing and had profited from it. But He threw out the one who hid the talent, telling him:

> You wicked servant! Shouldn't you have put my money in the bank? Then when I returned I would have at least got it back with interest. Take, therefore, the talent away from him and give it to the one who has ten. For the one who made good use of what he has been given shall receive more and he shall have an even greater abundance. But even what he has shall be taken away from the one who is unfaithful. And throw the useless servant into outer darkness, where there is weeping and gnashing of teeth (Matt. 25:26–30).

The point is that it is not His will for the grace we have received to be useless. Oh no, He *expects* us, as a duty, to give back to Him His own fruits, as St. Paul says, "The fruit of the Spirit is love, joy, and peace . . ." (Gal. 5:22).

Paul, being honorable and not owing anyone anything, but rather giving everything to everyone, was a true teacher of the

Lord's purpose in this matter. Thus he said, for example, "Pay everyone what is due to them" (Rom. 13:7). In that respect he was like those sent by the landowner (Matt. 21:33ff.) to receive the fruits of the vineyard from the farmers, because he urged everyone to make a proper return to God. Israel, as we know, despised the Lord and would not give a proper return. Their attitudes were not good—so bad, in fact, that they killed those He sent. Further, they did not even show reverence to the Lord of the vineyard, for they killed Him also.

THE BARREN FIG TREE CURSED

So when the Lord came and found Israel fruitless, He cursed them through the miracle of the fig tree, in which He said, "From now on let there be no fruit from you" (Matt. 21:19). That fig tree died fruitless, so quickly in fact that even His disciples were amazed when they saw that it had withered. Thus, the words of the prophet were fulfilled: "I will take away from them the voice of joy and the voice of gladness, the voice of the bridegroom and the voice of the bride, the scent of myrrh and the light of a lamp, and the whole land shall be destroyed" (Jer. 25:10).

The whole service of the ceremonial law has been taken away from them, and from now on and forever they do not have a feast. They do not observe the Passover—how can they? They no longer have a country of their own, but wander everywhere. And although they eat unleavened bread on the day set for the feast, they are not fulfilling the Law, because they are not able to properly sacrifice a lamb, as they were commanded to do. No, everywhere they make the attempt they break the Law, and God punishes them so that their "feast" days are days of grief instead of gladness.

There is one reason why this happened to them: They did not worship the Only-Begotten, but killed Him. In our time the wicked heretics and the ignorant schismatics are in the same boat: the former because they slay the Word (Christ the Son) and the latter because they divide the church. Both these groups are also outside the true Feast, because godliness and knowledge are missing from their lives. They imitate the conduct of the Jews in the matter of Bar Abbas the robber. Remember that they preferred him to the Savior. No wonder the Lord cursed them under the figure or type of the fig tree (Matt. 21:19)!

Yet in His lovingkindness He spared them, not destroying them root and all. You all recall that He did not curse the *root*, but said that no one would ever again eat *fruit* from it. When He did this, He abolished the pictures and shadows provided by the Jewish ceremonial law, and the whole system began to wither. But He preserved the root, so that we could be grafted in. And St. Paul says, "They, too, if they do not persist in their unbelief, can be grafted back into their own olive tree" (Rom. 11:23). Nevertheless, when the Lord condemned them because of their negligence, He took away their feasts, the value of the sacrificial lamb, and the true Passover.

But all that they lost was passed on to us! And along with it came the special, appointed day on which we are called to the Feast "with a trumpet," so to speak. For on this day we dedicate ourselves to the Lord with great thanksgiving, accepting it as our own Feast Day. We are committed to celebrating it, not for ourselves but for and to the Lord. Yea, and we rejoice not in ourselves but in the Lord, who bore our sorrows, and under the weight of them said, "My soul is sorrowful to the point of death" (Matt. 26:38).

The heathen, and indeed all who do not possess our faith, set up feasts according to their own ideas and plans. Consequently they have no peace, because they are living in sin against God. But the saints, those who belong to the Lord, keep His feasts just as they live for Him. They say, "I will rejoice in Your salvation," and "My soul shall be joyful in the Lord" (Ps. 35:9). And yes, they keep the commandment that says, "Rejoice in the Lord, O you righteous!" (Ps. 33:1). Thus, when gathered together, they all sing that festal Psalm, "Come, let us rejoice," not in ourselves, but "in the Lord" (Ps. 95:1).

LESSONS FROM THE SACRIFICE OF ISAAC

In the same way, the patriarch Abraham rejoiced at being able to see the day of the Lord — not some special day of his own. And as one who longed to see that day come, "he saw it, and was glad" (John 8:56).

Here is a man of true faith, for when the Lord asked him to sacrifice Isaac, his only son, he was willing to do so. By faith he offered up the one through whom the Lord had given him the promise of a nation of descendants (Heb. 11:17). And in offering his son he worshiped the Son of God. When the Lord held him back from sacrificing Isaac, Abraham saw the Messiah in the ram that was ultimately offered as the sacrifice to God (Gen. 22:13).

We see, then, that the patriarch was tested by means of Isaac — not that Isaac was sacrificed, but rather the One who was pointed out in Isaiah, "He shall be led as a lamb to the slaughter, and as a sheep before her shearers he shall be speechless" (Isa. 53:7). He was, in truth, tested by Him who took away the sin of the world.

That is why Abraham was held back from laying his hand on the boy. If he had sacrificed Isaac, the Jews might very well have rejected all the prophecies concerning the Savior. Undoubtedly they would have especially rejected such prophecies given by the psalmist as, "You have not wanted sacrifice and offering; for You have prepared a body for Me" (Ps. 40:6). They would have referred all such prophecies to the son of Abraham.

THE SACRIFICES COMPARED

Thus the sacrifice was not for the sake of Isaac but for that of Abraham, who was tested by being called upon to make this offering. And of course, God accepted his intentions, but He prevented him from slaying Isaac. The death of Isaac would not buy freedom for the world. Nay, that could be accomplished only by the death of our Savior, by whose stripes we are all healed (Isa. 53:5). He alone picked up the falling, healed the sick, satisfied those who were hungry, and filled the poor. Above all else, He alone raised us all from the dead, and having abolished death, He has brought us from sorrow and sighing to the rest and gladness of this Feast.

That, dear friends, is a joy that reaches heaven!

THE HEAVENLY CHURCH JOINS IN THE FESTIVAL

We are not alone in our joy, for in heaven the whole "church of the first-born" (Heb. 12:23) rejoices with us. As the ancient prophet put it, "Rejoice, O heavens, for the Lord has comforted Israel! Shout, foundations of the earth! Cry out with joy, O mountains, forests and all trees in them, for the Lord has redeemed Jacob and Israel has been glorified" (Isa. 44:23). And in another place he says, "Rejoice and be glad, you heavens; let the hills join in the gladness, for the Lord has had mercy on His people and has comforted the oppressed" (Isa. 49:13).

So you see, my friends, the whole creation keeps feast with us. As the psalmist says, everything that has breath praises the Lord (Ps. 150:6), both on account of the destruction of the Lord's enemies, and on account of our salvation.

That is quite appropriate, you know. For if there is joy in heaven over just one sinner repenting, can you imagine the celebration over the abolition of sin and the resurrection of the dead? Can you picture what kind of a joyful feast there must be in heaven?

Just think how the great multitude there shout jubilantly as they happily watch us in our gathering together—not only our weekly meetings but especially at Easter! For they see sinners who repented, people who changed when they were converted. They see people who at one time totally indulged their appetites and desires, yet are now humbling themselves by temperance and fasting.

But that is not all they see, for before their eyes lies the enemy, weakened, no longer possessing life, being bound hand and foot—so that they, along with us, may mock him, "Where is your victory, O Death? Where is your sting, O Grave?" (1 Cor. 15:55). So then, let us sing a victorious song of praise to the Lord!

Who will lead us to such a company of angels? Who, longing for the heavenly feast and the angels' holiday, will say like the prophet, "I will lead them to the house of God: a multitude joyfully praising God and keeping festival" (Ps. 42:4)? The saints of old encourage us to be like that, saying, for example, "Come let us go up to the mountain of the Lord, and to the house of the God of Jacob" (Isa. 2:3).

Such a feast as this is not for impure people, nor should sinners plan to be there. It is for virtuous and persistent people who have the same goal as the ancient saints. For, "Who shall ascend to the hill of the Lord? or who shall stand in His holy place? He who has clean hands and a pure heart. He who has not given his soul over to falsehood and has not sworn deceitfully to his neighbor. For he," the psalmist adds, when he goes to the holy place, "shall receive a blessing from the Lord" (Ps. 24:3–5). This, of course, clearly refers to what the Lord gives to those at His right hand when He says, "Come, you who are blessed by My Father, inherit the kingdom prepared for you" (Matt. 25:34).

But deceitful people with impure hearts, having nothing pure about them (as Proverbs 13:13 says, "To a deceitful man there is nothing good"), shall not be considered worthy to eat the Passover. They are foreigners, of a different race from the people of the Lord's church, and "a foreigner shall not eat of it" (Exod. 12:43). Thus Judas, even though he thought he was keeping the Passover, was actually alienated from the apostles and the heavenly city because he conspired against the Savior. The Law, you see, commanded that the Passover should be eaten with attention to its meaning. But he, even while he ate it, was "sifted by the devil" (cf. Luke 22:31), who had entered his soul.

MOSES, DAVID, AND DANIEL

Therefore, let us not just keep the Feast on earth, but rather in heaven with the angels. Let us glorify the Lord by temperance, by righteousness, and by those other virtues that go with them. And let us rejoice—not in ourselves, but in the Lord—so that we may be co-heirs with the saints.

Let us keep the Feast as Moses did. Let us watch through the day and night like David, who seven times a day (Ps. 119:164) and in the middle of the night gave thanks for the righteous judgments of God. And let us be early, as David said, "In the morning I will stand before You and You will see me and You will hear my voice" (Ps. 5:3). Let us fast like Daniel. Let us pray without ceasing as Paul commanded, all of us carrying out the times of prayers, especially those who are honorably married.

Then, when we have used these things to properly prepare ourselves for the Feast and have learned what we should from them, we will be ready to enter into the joy of our Lord in the kingdom of heaven.

THE LENTEN FAST: A PREPARATORY PURIFICATION

Israel, on its way to Jerusalem, was purified in the wilderness —trained to forget the customs of Egypt. Similarly, the Word has graciously prescribed the holy fast of forty days for us. Let us make it a time of purification and purging, so that after the fast we will be prepared to go to the upper room (cf. Luke 22:12–16) and eat with Him—and indeed to be partakers of the joys of heaven. There is no other way for us to be prepared to go up to Jerusalem and eat the Passover but to apply ourselves to the forty-day fast.

THE DATES OF THE EASTER SEASON

We begin the forty-day fast on February 25, fasting every day except Saturday and Sunday until March 31. Palm Sunday is April 1, and of course the following week is part of the fast, which comes to an end late in the evening of Saturday, April 6.[2] Then comes Easter Sunday (April 7), from which the glorious light of the grace of Christ shines all through the seven festal weeks to Pentecost Sunday. When we rest on that day, we will have completed the Feast of Easter by our observance of the

[2]At that time neither Saturdays nor Sundays were fast days during Lent, with the exception of the day before Easter. The fast was usually ended shortly before midnight on the day before Easter.

whole season. And all this by the grace of our Lord Jesus Christ, through whom, to the Father, be glory and dominion forever and ever. Amen.

All the brothers and sisters who are with me greet you. Greet one another with a holy kiss.

THE SEVENTH LETTER

A.D. 335

SINNERS CONTRASTED WITH THE RIGHTEOUS

INTRODUCTION TO THE SEVENTH LETTER

Athanasius here turns evangelist, writing a strong message of contrasts, comparing the condition — now and forever — of the wicked with that of the righteous. Not only do the wicked miss the blessed privilege of knowing the Lord, but they are making themselves miserable. And in the end, "the wicked shall be turned into hell."

But what a contrast to all this are the real followers of virtue who are confident in the Savior! Only they can glorify God in the way that it is meant to be done in a holy day. Only those who live in union with Christ can praise and bless God. So if wicked people keep the Easter Feast and speak words of praise, God rebukes them and calls all those beautiful words evil.

Athanasius pictures a distinct chasm between the wicked and the good. Those who do not seek the true Bread — Christ the Lord — cannot keep the Feast. The fact is that whatever they eat, and however much, they will never be satisfied. Ah, but to the one who belongs to Christ, "as the Scripture has said, out of his heart will flow rivers of living water" (John 7:38). Yes, the lives of God's people are fulfilled here and now, and in the end they inherit eternal life.

Now consider, says Athanasius, the parable of the prodigal son. His father took him back as a son, and with great rejoicing. Thus, the wicked can be assured that if they come to God, if they repent, then God will satisfy their hunger and thirst. They will inherit eternal life.

Today we seem so preoccupied with the benevolence of God that we can think only of calling people to experience His love. But sinners will not respond to God's love without understanding what they are leaving as well as what they are coming to. After all, there is everlasting punishment for the wicked, so they had better repent!

As I read this letter by Athanasius, I was reminded of a clear and strong statement by John of Damascus four centuries later:

> And the Devil and his demons, and his man, which is to say, the Antichrist, and the impious and sinners will be given over to everlasting fire, which will not be a material fire such as we are accustomed to, but a fire such as God might know. And those who have done good will shine like the sun together with the angels unto eternal life with our Lord Jesus Christ, ever seeing Him and being seen, enjoying the unending bliss which is from Him, and praising Him together with the Father and the Holy Ghost unto endless ages of ages. Amen.[1]

Yes, that is the message we need today. You who are far off, return, and you shall receive life and the kingdom from our Lord Jesus Christ.

Blessed Lamb! On Calvary's mountain
Slain to take our sin away:
Let the drops of that rich fountain
Our tremendous ransom pay!
Sacred Savior! Sacred Savior!
Humbly at thy feet we pray.

Blessed Lamb! Vouchsafe us pardon,
In thy love our souls confide:
By thy groans within the garden
By the death which thou hast died,
Let thy Passion—let thy Passion
Evermore with us abide!

[1]*The Orthodox Faith*, Book 4, Ch. 26, Fathers of the Church series, Vol. 37, (Washington, D.C.: Fathers of the Church, Inc., 1958).

So shall peace, sweet peace be given,
Purchase of thy precious pain;
So shall earth but lead to heaven,
Since for us the Lamb was slain:
Dear Redeemer! Dear Redeemer!
Thou canst not have died in vain.

—M. Bridges
(1800–1894)

LETTER VII

A.D. 335

Saint Paul wrote to the Corinthians that he always bore in his body the death of Jesus (2 Cor. 4:10). And he did not say it as if only he could make that boast, but also they, and we as well.[2] Let us, then, follow St. Paul in this: Let it be the regular boast of all of us all the time. David participated in it, for he said in the Psalms, "For your sake we die all day long; we are considered sheep for the slaughter" (Ps. 44:22).

This attitude is good for us, especially at the time of the Easter Feast, when our Savior's death is celebrated. For a person who has become like Him in His death also takes care to live as he should. He has the members of his body under control, so that they are dead to evil lusts (Col. 3:5). Such a person lives in the Spirit and is in harmony with the Spirit (cf. Gal. 5:25). He pays attention to God, never forgetting Him, and never participating in the works of death.

That is why St. Paul, wanting us to bear in our bodies the death of Jesus, immediately adds concerning such fellowship, "having the same spirit of faith as is described in the words 'I believed, therefore I spoke,' we also speak according to what we believe" (2 Cor. 4:13). Then he adds, speaking of the grace that comes from knowing the Lord, "For He that raised up Jesus will also raise us up with Jesus and will present us before Him with you" (2 Cor. 4:14).

[2]Those of us who have been baptized into Christ "have been buried with Him through baptism into death" and "united with Him in the likeness of His death" (Rom. 6:3–11).

THE WICKED AND THE GOOD

When, by such faith and knowledge, the Lord's people have embraced this true life, they surely receive the joy of heaven. The wicked, on the other hand, since they don't care about the Lord's life, are rightly deprived of its blessings. For, "let the wicked be taken away so that he shall not see the glory of the Lord" (Isa. 26:10, Septuagint). In the end they, like everyone else, shall hear the universal proclamation of the promise, "Awake, sleeper, and rise up from the dead" (Eph. 5:14). They shall rise and knock on the doors of heaven, saying, "Open to us" (Matt. 25:11). The Lord, however, will rebuke them for rejecting knowledge of Him, and will tell them, "I do not know you" (Luke 13:25). And the Holy Spirit speaks against them, "The wicked shall be turned into hell, and all the nations that forget God" (Ps. 9:17).

We may say of the wicked that they are indeed dead. They are not, however, dead in the same way that the Lord's people are — by a discipline opposed to sin. For they do not bear the Lord's death in their bodies as His people do. Instead, they bury their souls in sins and foolishness, feeding them on things that are dead. They are like young eagles that dive down upon the carcasses of the dead and eat them. The Law, you will recall, pronounced everything unclean that eats the dead: "You shall not eat the eagle nor any other bird which feeds on a dead carcass" (Lev. 11:13). In that command there was a figurative directive against those who do things that will kill their souls.

But these wicked people go right on killing their souls with all kinds of lusts. They just say, "Let's eat and drink, for tomorrow we die" (Isa. 22:13). The prophet Isaiah described the fruit of such pleasure-loving lives: "But the Lord of Hosts has revealed these things to me: that this sin will not be forgiven you till you die" (Isa. 22:14). Yes, even while they live they shall be ashamed, because they consider their belly their lord. And when they die, they shall be tormented for having made such a boast about death.

Paul also told us the same thing: "Food is for the belly and the belly for food, but God shall destroy both" (1 Cor. 6:13).

And long ago, the Holy Scriptures declared concerning the wicked, "The death of sinners is evil, and those who hate the righteous commit sin" (Ps. 34:21). Evil people inherit a bitter worm and a tragic darkness.

But the saints, the real followers of goodness, "make the members of their earthly bodies dead to fornication, impurity, wicked passions, and evil desire" (Col. 3:5). As a result they are pure and spotless, trusting in the promise of our Savior, who told us, "Blessed are the pure in heart, for they shall see God" (Matt. 5:8). Having become dead to the world and having renounced all its goods, they come to an honorable end, for "precious in the sight of the Lord is the death of His saints" (Ps. 116:15).

Further, the saints are able, like St. Paul, to say, "I am crucified with Christ, nevertheless I live; yet not I, but Christ lives in me" (Gal. 2:20). Real life is a life lived in Christ. And although the Lord's people are dead to the world, they live, as it were, in heaven. They think about those things which are above. As one lover of heaven put it, "While we walk on earth, our dwelling is in heaven."[3]

Those who live that way and participate in such goodness are the only ones able to give glory to God—and that is what really constitutes a feast and a holiday. For the Feast is not indulging in a lot of food, nor dressing up in lovely clothes, nor enjoying days of leisure. It is acknowledging God and offering thanksgivings and songs of praise to Him.

SINNERS CANNOT OBSERVE THE FESTIVAL

But this applies only to the saints, to those who live in Christ. For it is written, "The dead shall not praise You, O Lord, nor any of those who go down to hell; but we who live will bless the Lord, from now on forever" (Ps. 115:17,18). That's the way it was with Hezekiah, who praised the Lord because he was delivered from death: "Those who are in hell cannot praise You; the dead

[3]This statement is not an exact quote of any Scripture, but it captures the thought of St. Paul in Phil. 3:17–20.

cannot bless You; but the living shall bless You, as I do today" (Isa. 38:18, 19).

Only those who live in Christ can praise and bless God, and it is by means of this that they go up to the Feast. The Passover does not belong to the Gentiles nor to those who are Jews in the flesh, but rather to those who acknowledge the truth in Christ. That acknowledgment is given in St. Paul's proclamation, "Our Passover, Christ, is sacrificed" (1 Cor. 5:7).

So although wicked men keep the Feast and even praise God and intrude into the church of the saints, God rejects them. For He asks, "Why do you talk of my laws?" (Ps. 50:16). And the gentle Spirit rebukes them, saying, "Praise is not pretty in the mouth of a sinner."[4] Sin simply does not have anything in common with the praise of God. The sinner, however, cannot help saying wicked things. As the Proverb puts it, "The mouth of the wicked pours out evil things" (Prov. 15:28).

How could we possibly praise God with an impure mouth when things that are contrary to each other cannot exist in the same person? As that great minister of the gospel, St. Paul, asked, "What communion is there between righteousness and iniquity? What fellowship is there between light and darkness?" (2 Cor. 6:14).

Consider, then, the case of sinners and everyone else who is alien to the catholic church, such as heretics and schismatics. Since they are excluded from taking part in the praise and thanksgiving made by the saints, it isn't proper for them even to continue to be observers of the Feast. On the other hand, the righteous man, even though in the eyes of the world he is dying, says simply, "I shall not die, but live and tell all Your marvelous deeds" (Ps. 118:17). For God is not ashamed to be called the God (Heb. 11:16) of those who put to death the members of their earthly bodies (Col. 3:5), but who live in Christ. He is, after all, the God of the living, not of the dead.

And He, by His living Word (Christ the Son), gives life to everyone, and gives Him to be food and life to the saints. That is why the Lord exclaimed, "I am the bread of Life!" (John

[4]Ecclus. 15:9.

6:48). The Jews, unable to understand, having minds unused to goodness, and not being ready to accept the Bread He talked about, spoke out against Him because He said, "I am the living bread which came down from heaven and gives life to men" (John 6:51).

CHRIST TRULY SATISFIES THE BELIEVER'S DESIRES

Sin, you know, has her own special "bread," too—the bread of her death. Therefore she calls to those who love pleasure and lack discernment, " 'Touch with delight secret bread, and sweet waters which are stolen' " (Prov. 9:17). The person who merely touches them is not aware that people who are bound to earthly things perish along with sin.

But alas! Even when the sinner looks for gratification, he doesn't find the fruit of his sin pleasant. As the wisdom of God says in another place, "Bread of deceit is pleasant to a man, but after he eats it, his mouth will be filled with gravel" (Prov. 20:17). And, "Honey drips from the lips of an adulteress, and for a time it tastes sweet, but in the end you will find it more bitter than gall and sharper than a two-edged sword" (Prov. 5:3,4). So he eats and is quite pleased for a little while. Then, when it is too late, when he has cut off his soul from God, he rejects it. But the fool does not know that those who are cut off from God shall perish.

Because of this the prophet, attempting to keep the sinner from going too far, warned, "What are you doing on the road to Egypt, to drink the waters of the Nile? And what are you doing on the road to Assyria, to drink the waters of the Euphrates?" (Jer. 2:18). And the wisdom of God, who loves mankind, also issues a prohibition, "But depart quickly, do not tarry in the place, nor fix your eye upon it; for in that way you shall pass over strange waters and depart quickly from the strange river."[5]

She (wisdom) then calls people to herself. "Wisdom has built

[5]This quotation is from Prov. 9:18 in the LXX (Septuagint) version. It is not found in the Hebrew version.

her house and supported it on seven pillars; she has killed her sacrifices and mixed her wine and prepared her table; she has sent out her servants, loudly calling people to the table, saying, 'Whoever is naive, come to me.' And to people who lack understanding, she says, 'Come and eat of my bread and drink of the wine I have mixed for you' " (Prov. 9:1–5).

And what does wisdom expect in return? "Forsake your folly and live, and seek understanding that you may continue to do so" (Prov. 9:6). For the bread which wisdom gives is living food, as the Lord said, "I am the living bread which came down from heaven: if anyone eats this bread, he will live forever" (John 6:51). When the people of Israel ate manna, even though it was very good and quite nourishing, they still died. Not one of those who ate it lived forever as a result; all of them died in the wilderness. In contrast, the Lord says, "I am the bread of life. Your fathers ate manna in the wilderness and are dead. This is the bread which came down from heaven so that people could eat it and not die" (cf. John 6:48–51).

Even wicked people want that kind of bread, for sick souls *do* hunger. But only the righteous, being prepared for it, will be satisfied and able to say, "I shall behold Your face in righteousness; I shall be satisfied when I see Your glory" (Ps. 17:15). A person who has once eaten divine bread always wants more, and anyone who has such a hunger receives a never-failing gift, as wisdom promises: "The Lord will not allow the soul of the righteous to hunger" (Prov. 10:3).

There is a similar promise in the Psalms: "I will abundantly bless her provision; I will satisfy her poor with bread" (Ps. 132:15). And then, in the Gospels we hear our Savior saying, "Blessed are they who hunger and thirst after righteousness, for they shall be filled" (Matt. 5:6).

Thus it is a good thing that the saints, those who love life in Christ, build up a longing for this kind of food. One of them earnestly requested, "As the deer pants for the water brooks, my soul pants for You, O God. My soul thirsts for the living God. When shall I come and see the face of God?" (Ps. 42:1). And, "My God, my God, I seek You early; my soul thirsts for You; my flesh yearns for You in a dry and pathless land where there is no water. Thus, I came before You in holiness to see Your Power and Your glory" (Ps. 63:1,2).

With this in mind, dear friends, let us subdue the appetites of the members of our bodies (Col. 3:5) and receive nourishment from the Living Bread by faith and love to God, for we know that without faith it is impossible to be partakers of this Bread. Our Savior, when He called everyone to Himself, said, "If any man thirst, let him come to Me and drink" (John 7:37). Then He immediately spoke of the faith that is necessary if we are to actually receive such food: "He who believes on Me, as the Scripture says, out of his innermost being shall flow rivers of living water" (John 7:38).

Remember also that He continually nourished His believing disciples with His words and gave them life by His closeness. But when the woman from Canaan asked for help, he didn't answer her (Matt. 15:22,23) because she was not yet a believer —even though she desperately needed food from Him! He did not behave this way because He despised her; far from it. For the Lord is loving and good to mankind. That's why He went to Tyre and Sidon in the first place. No, it was because she did not believe, because she was an impious woman who had no idea of God's requirements.

What He did was most appropriate, brothers and sisters, because it wasn't right for her to put her request before faith. Rather, she needed to support her prayer by her faith. For "he who comes to God must first believe that He is, and that He is a rewarder of those who seek Him; and that without faith it is impossible to please Him" (Heb. 11:6). That is what Paul teaches.[6]

The Lord shows that this woman was an unbeliever, an unholy person up to that point, when He says, "It is not right to take the children's bread and throw it to dogs" (Matt. 15:26). At that point she was convinced by the power of the Word, and thus having abandoned her unholy condition, she acquired faith. Then the Lord no longer treated her like a dog, but talked

[6]Athanasius apparently considered St. Paul to be the author of the Letter to the Hebrews.

with her as a human being, saying, "O woman, great is your faith!" (Matt. 15:28). Thus, when she believed He immediately granted her the fruit of that faith, saying, " 'It will be done as you wish.' And her daughter was healed immediately" (Matt. 15:28).

CHRIST: FOOD OF THE ANGELS

The righteous person, fed by faith and knowledge and doing what the Lord commands, always has a healthy soul. That is why we are commanded to "accept the one who is weak in faith" (Rom. 14:1), even if he isn't able to eat bread yet, but can only take vegetables ("for he who is weak eats only vegetables"). Even the Corinthians couldn't handle such bread, because they were babes, and like babes they drank milk (cf. 1 Cor. 3:1). For, according to the godly writer, "everyone who partakes only of milk is unable to handle the word of righteousness" (Heb. 5:13).

The apostle Paul, in his first letter to his beloved son Timothy, urges him "to be nourished with the word of faith and the good teaching which he had been following" (1 Tim. 4:6). And in his second letter, "Hold to the example of the sound words which I taught you, in the faith and love which are in Christ Jesus" (2 Tim. 1:13).

Dear friends, it is not only here that the Bread is the food of the righteous. Nor are the saints on earth the only ones who are nourished by such Bread and such blood. We shall eat them in heaven, for the Lord is the food also of the exalted spirits and of the angels. Indeed, He is the joy of the whole heavenly host. He is everything to all and He spares all according to His lovingkindness. The Lord has already given us angels' food, and He gives a great promise to those who stand with Him in His trials: "As my Father has promised Me a kingdom, I promise to you that you shall eat and drink at My table in My kingdom and sit on twelve thrones, judging the twelve tribes of Israel" (Luke 22:29,30).

Oh, brothers and sisters, what a banquet that is! And how great is the harmony and joy of those who eat at this heavenly table! They enjoy food which produces life everlasting, not that ordinary food which passes right on through the body. Who will be considered worthy to be in that group? Who is so blessed as to be called to and counted worthy of that divine feast? For "blessed is he who shall eat bread in your kingdom" (Luke 14:15). But even a person who has been judged worthy of this heavenly calling and has been sanctified by it can, although he has been washed, become unclean. How? "Counting as unclean the blood of the covenant by which he was sanctified and despising the Spirit of grace" (Heb. 10:29), he hears the Lord say, "Friend, how did you get in here without wedding garments?" (Matt. 22:12).

The banquet of the saints, you see, is pure and spotless, for "many are called, but few are chosen" (Matt. 22:14). Judas, for example, thought very little of the Supper even though he came to it. So he left the Lord's presence and, having abandoned his life (cf. Col. 3:4), he hanged himself. Oh, but the disciples who remained with the Redeemer also shared in the happiness of the Feast.

THE PRODIGAL SON'S HOMECOMING

Consider, however, the case of that young man who went to a faraway country and wasted his inheritance by riotous living. If he comes to his right mind and decides he wants this divine Feast, he will say, "How many of my father's servants have bread to spare, while I perish here with hunger!" (Luke 15:17). Then he shall get up and come to his father and confess to him, "I have sinned against heaven and before you. I am no longer worthy to be called your son. Treat me like one of your hired servants" (Luke 15:18,19).

When he confesses like that, he shall be considered worthy of more than he prayed for. His father doesn't take him in like a hired servant, nor treat him like a stranger! Oh no, he kisses him as a son. He accepts him as a dead man come back to life again, counts him worthy of the divine Feast, and gives him the precious garment he once wore.

And now there is singing and joy in the father's home. For what has happened is the result of the Father's grace and lovingkindness. Not only does He bring his son back from death, but through the Spirit He clearly shows His grace. To replace corruption, He clothes him with an incorruptible garment. To satisfy hunger, He kills the fatted calf. And the Father provides shoes for his feet so that he will not travel far away again. And most wonderful of all, He puts a divine signet ring upon his hand. By all these things He begets him anew in the image of the glory of Christ.

EXHORTATION TO SINNERS

These, then, are the gracious gifts of the Father by which the Lord honors and nourishes those who abide with Him — and also those who repent and come back to Him. He promises, "I am the bread of life . . . he who comes to Me shall never thirst" (John 6:35). We, too, can be counted worthy of these things. We need only to maintain purity and cling to our Savior — not just in the six days of Easter, but considering the whole course of life as a feast, remain near Him, saying, "You have the words of eternal life, where else can we go?" (John 6:68).

So if any of us are far off, let us come back now, confessing our sins, holding nothing against anyone, and by the Spirit crushing evil desire and killing its deeds (Rom. 8:13). In that way, having nourished the soul while we are here, we shall partake with angels at that heavenly and spiritual table. We will not knock and be sent away like those five foolish virgins (Matt. 25:1–12), but we shall enter with the Lord, like those who were wise and loved the bridegroom. Showing the death of Jesus in our bodies (2 Cor. 4:10), we shall receive life and the kingdom from Him.

THE DATES OF THE FAST AND FEAST

We begin the fast of forty days on February 17 and the Easter Week fast on March 24. Then, as we are able, let us fast and watch and pray through those last six days, breaking the fast on Saturday evening, March 29. Then when that day which is holy and blessed in everything, possessing the name of Christ—the Lord's Day—comes (March 30) we shall begin the Feast, which lasts until Pentecost Sunday. Let us, then, at all times worship the Father through Christ, by whom to Him and with Him be glory and dominion by the Holy Spirit forever and ever. Amen.

All the brothers and sisters who are with me greet you. Greet one another with a holy kiss.

THE EIGHTH LETTER

A.D. 338

PRAISE THE LORD IN DIFFICULTIES

INTRODUCTION TO THE EIGHTH LETTER

This is the Festal Letter for Athanasius' *tenth* year. We have no trace of the letters for the eighth and ninth years. The ancient chronicles said he could not write them because of his troubles, and this may well be the case, although it is likely that he sent a brief notice of the dates, at least. He was summoned to a council at Tyre (summer of 335) where enemies outnumbered friends. We have told earlier of how he fled to Constantinople and was exiled to Gaul. He was still in exile there when he began this letter of 338, finishing it after he had returned home.

Many things are dealt with here. Athanasius starts with a thanksgiving for deliverance from his troubles and then tells of how God deals with each one of us according to our needs. He points out that no place is really a desert for the faithful, and there are no difficulties so bad that we should get greatly upset. After all, as Paul says, we have Christ to strengthen us, and we are more than conquerors through Him (Rom. 8:37).

The difficulties through which Athanasius had been passing were obviously in his mind as he wrote these things. Trials and tribulations had matured him, and he passed his thoughts on to the flock. Then his thoughts turned to the Arian heretics, and he wrote of how damaging was their wrong teaching of Jesus Christ. Since they would not have Him to be truly God, they robbed themselves of salvation. Therefore, they persecuted the people of God.

But what of the believers? In view of all this, what should

they do? Keep the Feast, says Athanasius. Give praise and thanks to God. Oh yes, he says, these enemies of Christ have put me through the wringer, but they haven't defeated Him and His holy church. So let's keep the holy day, just as we always have.

It seems that the dangers are more subtle today. Sure, we have enemies of Christ around, dressed in all kinds of clothes, many cleverly disguised as Christians. We are not, however, being exiled or tortured or killed for clinging to the truth concerning the Savior. So there's a tendency to live and let live, to join ourselves with all who profess to be Christians, no matter what their doctrine is. The fact is that false doctrines are as dangerous as ever. Let us not be guilty of reconciling truth with falsehood. Let us not be drawn into fellowship with darkness. Instead, let us cling to the faith of our fathers, once for all delivered. And let us keep the Feast in sincerity and in truth.

LETTER VIII

A.D. 338

Although I have been all this distance away from you, brothers and sisters, I have not forgotten the custom that has been handed down to us by the Fathers. I shall not neglect to notify you of the season of the annual holy Feast and the day on which it is to be celebrated.

ATHANASIUS WATCHED BY HIS ENEMIES

It is true that I have been hindered by those hardships that you have probably heard about, and severe trials have been laid upon me. And we have been separated by a great distance. At the same time, the enemies of the truth have been watching us, laying traps to discover a letter from us. They have hoped that they could, by their accusations, make our wounds more painful. Nevertheless, the Lord has strengthened and comforted us in our afflictions. So we have not been afraid, even in the midst of such schemes and conspiracies, to send you word about our saving Easter Feast—even from the ends of the earth!

When I wrote to the presbyters of Alexandria, I urged them to send these letters to you, although I knew how our enemies would try to scare them. Still, I reminded them of the boldness of the apostle Paul's speech and asked them to remember that "Nothing separates us from the love of Christ, neither affliction, nor distress, nor persecution, nor famine, nor peril, nor sword" (Rom. 8:35). Keeping the Feast myself, I wanted you also, dear friends, to keep it. Therefore, knowing that an announcement like this is due from me, I have not held back from that duty, because I wanted to do the right thing, as Paul advised: "Render to everyone his due" (Rom. 13:7).

CHRIST THE BESTOWER OF THE SPIRIT

Although I committed all my affairs to God, I still wanted to celebrate the Feast with you, disregarding the distance between us. For although distance separates us, the Lord who gives the Feast is the Feast (1 Cor. 5:7). He bestows the Spirit, bringing us together in mind, in harmony, and in the bond of peace. When we turn our attention to the same things and offer up the same prayers on behalf of each other, no distance can divide us. The Lord gathers us together and unites us. We are promised that "when two or three are gathered together in His name, He is in the midst of them" (Matt. 18:20).

Plainly, then, since He is in the midst of all His churches meeting everywhere, He unites them and accepts all their prayers as if they were in the same place. Yes, He hears them all as they cry out the same "Amen!"

THANKSGIVING AFTER DELIVERANCE FROM AFFLICTION

That is the way in which I have looked at the hardships and trials I mentioned when I wrote to you, dear friends. And so that we do not make things painful for you, I just want to give you a brief reminder here. It isn't right, you know, for a person to forget, when things get easier, the pains he experienced under tribulation — lest he be excluded from the divine company as a forgetful and unthankful person.

There is no time more appropriate for a person to have a thankful attitude toward God than when he has been going through tribulations and hardships. Nor is there a better time to be giving thanks than when he has come to rest after struggles and temptations. A good example is King Hezekiah, who praised the Lord and gave Him thanks after Israel's Assyrian enemies perished: "The Lord is my salvation, and I will not cease to praise Thee with harp all the days of my life, before the house of the Lord" (Isa. 38:20).

Or consider those three saintly men who went through a tremendous trial in Babylon: Hananiah, Mishael, and Azariah (cf. Dan. 1–3). When they saw they were safe and the fire was more like dew than danger, these men gave thanks, singing a song to God.[1] Brothers and sisters, I, like them, have written with all that I have been through in mind. For in our own time God has made things happen that would be impossible for human beings to do. Things which men could never accomplish He has shown to be easy for Him — for example, bringing us back to you.

For God has not given us over as victims to those who are out to swallow up not just us, but the whole church — who are trying by their wickedness to overwhelm faith and godliness. Oh yes, that is what they had in mind. But God, who is good, showed us His lovingkindness over and over again. Not only did He give us salvation through His Word (Christ the Son), but now He has rescued us from those enemies who persecuted us and planned to destroy us. As St. Paul once said when he was describing the unbelievable riches of Christ: "But God, being rich in mercy, because of the great love with which He loved us even when we were dead in foolishness and sins, made us alive through Christ" (Eph. 2:4,5).

Ultimately, the power of men and of all creatures is weak and miserable. But the eternal, uncreated Might is rich and incomprehensible, having no beginning and no end. It is so far above man that we cannot grasp it at all.

GOD'S DEALINGS WITH HUMANITY

God does not have just one means of healing. No, having unlimited resources, He works in many ways for our salvation by means of His Word, who is in no way restricted or hindered

[1] *The Song of the Three Children* is that addition to Daniel (between 3:23 and 3:24) found in the Greek, but not in the Hebrew, version of the Old Testament. It is part of those works called the *Apocrypha*, which were traditionally transmitted alongside the canonical Scriptures.

in His dealings with us. Rather, since He does have such infinite assets and is so absolutely versatile, He does for each of us exactly what we personally need. For He (Christ) is the Word, and the Power, and the Wisdom of God. And, as Solomon tells us concerning Wisdom, "being one, it can do all things, and remaining in itself, it makes all things new; and passing upon holy souls, fashions the friends of God and the prophets."[2]

To those who, like little lambs, have not yet reached maturity, there is milk, such as Paul fed some: "I have fed you with milk, not with meat" (1 Cor. 3:2). There is also appropriate food for those who have gone beyond babyhood to adolescence, but still are not quite mature. Of them Paul says, "Let him that is weak eat vegetables" (Rom. 14:2). But as soon as a person begins to behave like a mature and holy Christian, his diet changes and instead of being fed on these things, he has the Word (Christ) for bread and flesh for food, for the Scriptures say, "Solid food is for the mature, for those who have grown up enough to have their senses trained" (Heb. 5:14).

WE EACH RECEIVE THE GRACE WE NEED

There are other differences as well. When the Word is sown, it does not yield the same size crop in all human beings. Rather, the crop is varied and rich. In some the yield is a hundredfold, others sixty, and others thirty (Matt. 13:8), as the Savior, that Sower of grace and Bestower of the Spirit, teaches. And this isn't just something that *may* happen or something on which we have no confirmation. All we have to do is look at the field He has sown: In the church the Word has produced many different results and the product is rich and varied.

Nor, as some think, are only virgins or monks meant by the "field," but honorable matrimony and, indeed, the purity of all. For in sowing He does not force us to something beyond the abilities of our wills. Nor is the grace confined to those who are

[2]Wisdom 7:27.

fully mature. It passes down through all levels so that He can bring all people to salvation.

That is why He, along with the Father, has prepared many mansions (John 14:2). Although our dwelling places vary according to how far along we have come in the practice of the faith (cf. 2 Cor. 5:10), all of us are within the wall and we are all enclosed by the same fence. The devil and the whole host of his demons and followers are kept out. For apart from light there is darkness, and apart from blessing there is a curse. The devil is apart from the saints, just as sin is far from virtue. Therefore our Lord rebuked Satan, saying, "Get thee behind Me, Satan" (Matt. 4:10).

We, on the other hand, are called to the Lord: "Come, blessed of My Father, inherit the kingdom which is prepared for you" (Matt. 25:34). So, in the Psalms we hear the Spirit crying out to His people, "Enter into His gates with thanksgiving" (Ps. 100:4).

CHARACTERISTICS OF RIGHTEOUSNESS AND SIN

By means of righteousness we come into God's presence, as Moses did when he entered the thick cloud where God was (Exod. 19:20). On the other hand, by the practice of evil a person leaves the presence of the Lord. For example, Cain, when he killed his brother, left the Lord's presence as far as his will was concerned (Gen. 4:16). In contrast to that attitude, the psalmist comes to the Lord, saying, "And I will go in to the altar of God, to God who is the gladness of my joy" (Ps. 43:4).

But the devil! The Scripture tells us that he went out from God's presence and afflicted Job with painful boils (Job 2:7). After all, that is the characteristic of those who leave God: to find His people and afflict them in some way. The most distinguishing trait of those who fall away from the faith is that they set out to persecute and do harm to the faithful.

The saints, on the other hand, draw other faithful believers to themselves and consider them their friends. David put it clearly and plainly: "I look for the faithful of the earth, so that I can live with them" (Ps. 101:6). And Paul urges us to accept even those who are weak in the faith (Rom. 14:1). For righteous people love humanity, while sinners hate their fellow human beings. Thus the sinner Saul persecuted David; but although David had plenty of opportunity, he did not kill Saul. Esau persecuted Jacob, but Jacob tried to overcome his brother's wickedness by meekness. And although Joseph's eleven brothers sold him, he, in his lovingkindness, had pity on them.

THE PERVERSENESS OF THE JEWS

But why do we need a lot of words? When our Lord and Savior was persecuted by the Pharisees, He wept because of their coming destruction. He was treated badly, but He did not even make threats in return—neither when he was abused nor when He was killed. In fact, the opposite was true, for He grieved for those who dared to do such things. But they contemptuously shoved aside light and life and grace, which they could have had through the Savior, who suffered in our place.

It was actually for the darkness and blindness of such people that He wept. If they had understood the things written in the Psalms, they would never have been so brash as to undertake such futile attacks upon the Savior. For in the Psalms the Spirit said, "Why do the heathen rage, and the people imagine a vain thing?" (Ps. 2:1). And if they had considered the prophecy of Moses (Deut. 18:15; 28:66), they never would have hanged Him who was their life. Further, if they had applied their minds to what was written in the Scriptures, they would not have fulfilled so studiously the prophesies which were written about them. But they did, and in consequence their city lies desolate, grace has been taken away from them, and they don't have the Law anymore. God no longer calls them children, but strangers.

All those things they did were actually right there in the Scriptures before their eyes. The psalmist had predicted, "The strange children have acted falsely by Me" (Ps. 18:45, Septuagint). And Isaiah the prophet had said, "I have begotten and brought up children, and they have rejected Me" (Isa. 1:2).

They are no longer called the people of God and a holy nation, but rulers of Sodom and people of Gomorrah. They have gone beyond even the sin of the Sodomites, as the prophet foretold, "Sodom will be justified before you will" (cf. Ezek. 16:48; Lam. 4:6). For the Sodomites only attacked angels, but these people attacked the Lord and God and King of all and actually dared to kill the Lord of angels. They did not know that Christ, who was killed by them, would live yet today.

Those Jews who conspired against Him, however, having fallen away from eternal matters, had only a little while to rejoice in their temporal triumphs, and then they died. They were ignorant of the fact that the immortal promise is not with respect to temporary enjoyment, but relates to the hope of the life everlasting.

The saint of God goes through tribulations, hard work, and much sorrow on earth before entering into the kingdom of heaven. But when he gets to that place where sorrow and distress and longing disappear, he will enjoy eternal rest—as did Job, who faced many trials here but became the friend of the Lord. What a contrast to those who love pleasure and are actually able to rejoice in it for a short time, but end up having a sorrowful life. Esau is an example of them, for he enjoyed one short meal but was afterward condemned for his behavior.

NO PLACE IS A DESERT FOR THE FAITHFUL

We might compare these distinctions to the departures of the children of Israel and that of the Egyptians from Egypt. The Egyptians, briefly rejoicing in their unjust treatment of Israel, went out after them and were all drowned. But the people of God, though afflicted and persecuted for a little while by their taskmasters, went through the sea unharmed when they came out of Egypt (cf. Exod. 14). They lived in the desert as if it were an inhabited place; for although the place was desolate and nobody lived there, yet because of the gracious gift of the Law and communion with angels it was even better for them than an inhabited country.

Elisha (cf. 2 Kings 6:13–17), when he thought he was all alone in the wilderness, was really in the presence of hosts of angels. The people of Israel went from persecution to the wilderness, and those who remained faithful later entered the Promised Land.

In the same way, those people today who remain steadfast in the face of difficulties will go on to a place of comfort, while those who persecute others will be trampled underfoot and come to a bad end. For that conclusion we have the example of the rich man accurately described in the Gospel (Luke 16:19). He lived here in pleasure for a time, but he suffered hunger after he left this life. Having drunk as he pleased here, he was parched with thirst there. Lazarus, on the other hand, had many troubles and difficulties in his life in this world, but he found rest in heaven. Here he was hungry for ordinary bread, but there he was satisfied with bread better than manna.

For the Lord who came from there said, "I am the bread which came down from heaven and gives life to mankind" (John 6:51).

TEMPORAL ILLS NO REASON FOR DISTRESS

Oh, dear friends! The time is coming when we shall be comforted for all our troubles, when we shall rest from our hard work, when we shall regain our lost health, when after dying we shall have immortal life. Therefore, we shouldn't be too upset by all the problems we have as human beings in this life. It isn't right to be agitated by all the difficulties we run into. It isn't right to be afraid when the enemy host that fought against Christ conspires against godliness.

When these things come along, we should simply please God all the more by treating them as the trying and testing of a virtuous life. After all, how can we expect to develop patience if we haven't faced sorrow and hard work? Or how would we ever experience fortitude if our enemies never attacked us? How could we ever show courage if we never had to face bad treatment and injustice? Indeed, how would we ever expect to be long-suffering if we had not faced the opposition of antichrists?

And finally, how could a person hope to recognize virtue when he sees it if he has not actually seen the sin and iniquity of the wicked?

Our Lord and Savior Jesus Christ, therefore, is an example to us of how to suffer. When they struck Him, He bore it patiently; when they mocked Him and verbally abused Him, He didn't lash back at them; when He suffered, He didn't threaten His persecutors. Rather, He presented His back to those who wished to whip Him; He turned His cheeks to those who wished to slap Him; He didn't even turn His face away when they spat upon Him (1 Peter 2:23; Isa. 50:6). And at the end, He willingly let them lead Him to death, so that we could see in Him the picture of all that is good and immortal. Consequently, He is our example, and following Him we really can tread on serpents and scorpions—and on all the power of the enemy!

WE BENEFIT THROUGH TRIALS AND SUFFERINGS

So Paul, who followed the Lord's example, urged us, "Follow me, as I follow Christ" (1 Cor. 11:1). In so doing, the apostle had successfully overcome the devils' whole army so that he could write, "I am persuaded that neither death, nor life, nor angels, nor principalities, nor things present, nor things to come, nor powers, nor height, nor depth, nor any other creature, shall be able to separate us from the love of God which is in Jesus Christ" (Rom. 8:38,39).

Whenever we have suffering and troubles and hard work, the enemy comes along and does everything he can to make us fall. But the person who is in Christ can be victorious by setting himself against the opposition — meeting anger with long-suffering, insults with meekness, vice with virtue. Then he can triumphantly exclaim, "I can do all things through Christ who strengthens me" (Phil. 4:13). And, "In all these things we are conquerors through Christ who loved us" (Rom. 8:37).

That is the grace of the Lord. All these troubles and difficulties are the Lord's means of correcting and training the children of men. He suffered to buy freedom from suffering for those who suffer in Him, and He came down in order to raise us up. He went to the trouble of being born so that we would love Him who is unbegotten. He accepted a decaying body so that decaying bodies might put on immortality. He became weak for us that we might rise with power. He went down to death that He might give life to the dead, and give us immortal life.

In summary, He became man so that we who die as man might live again, that death should not reign over us anymore. As the apostle Paul proclaimed, "Death shall not have dominion over us" (Rom. 6:9).

THE ERRONEOUS OPINIONS OF THE ARIANS[3]

Since they do not care about these things, the Ario-maniacs, being heretics who oppose Christ, flail away at the Helper with their tongues and blaspheme the One who set us free.

Taking everything in the wrong way, they have departed from orthodoxy concerning the Redeemer. They take His becoming man, which after all was for the benefit of humanity, and use it to deny His true divinity. Taking note of the fact that He was born from the Virgin, they question His being truly the Son of God. Pointing out that He became incarnate in time, they deny His eternity. Seeing that He suffered for us, they renounce their faith in Him as the incorruptible Son from the incorruptible Father. And because He endured physical pain for our sakes, they deny that He could possibly be eternal.

Having become unthankful, they reject the Savior and insult Him instead of acknowledging His grace.

THE ARIANS MISUNDERSTOOD THE SCRIPTURES

It is appropriate for us to say to them: "Oh, unthankful enemy of Christ, utterly wicked killer of your Lord, mentally

[3]The Arians, you will recall, were the infamous fourth-century heretics who fought against the eternality of the Son, saying, for example, "There was a time when He was not."

blind and a Jew in your conscience! You should have understood the Scriptures and listened to the ancient saints, who said, 'Cause Your face to shine and we shall be saved' (Ps. 80:7) and, 'Send out Your light and Your Truth' (Ps. 43:3). Then you would have known that the Lord didn't come down on His own account, but on ours. As a result, you would have esteemed His lovingkindness so much more.

"And if you had thought about just who and what the Father is—and the Son as well—you would not have blasphemed the Son by saying He had a changeable nature.[4] If you had at all understood His works of lovingkindness for us, you would not have decided that the Son was different from the Father. Nor would you have considered the One who reconciled us to His Father to be a stranger to that Father."

THE ARIANS AND THE SCHISMATICS CONNECTED

I know that these words are hard to take, not only for those who downgrade Christ, but also for the schismatics. For these two groups are united in a way, having certain kindred feelings. Both have learned to "rend the seamless coat of God." That is, neither of them feels the least bit bad about separating the inseparable Son from the Father.

I also know that when they hear these words, they will gnash their teeth, as will the devil who stirs them up. And for just one reason: It bothers them to hear the truth about our Redeemer's glory. But the Lord, who has always scoffed at the devil, does the same now, saying as always, "I am in the Father, and the Father is in Me" (John 14:11). For He is the *Lord*, who is revealed in the Father—and in whom the Father is revealed. It is He who, although eternally the true Son of the Father, became incarnate in time for our sakes. He offered Himself to the Father in our place and redeemed us by His offering and sacrifice.

[4]One of the characteristics of God is that He is immutable, unchangeable. The Arians said the Son did not have this characteristic.

He is the One who long ago brought the people of Israel out of Egypt and then later redeemed all of us—the whole race of men—from death, saving us from the grave. He is the One who in ancient days was sacrificed as a lamb, for He was pictured in those lambs sacrificed by Israel. But later, He Himself was slain for us, for "Christ our Passover is sacrificed" (1 Cor. 5:7). He is the One who now has delivered us from the snare of the hunters. He threw out the opponents of Christ (the Arians) and the schismatics, and once again rescued us, His church. Because we were victimized by their deception, He Himself has rescued us.

ENEMIES OF THE CHURCH UNSUCCESSFUL

In the face of all this, brothers and sisters, what should we do but give thanks to God, the King of all? Let us start by crying out the words of the Psalm, "Blessed be the Lord, Who has not let them eat us up" (Ps. 124:6). Let us keep the Feast in that way which He has established for our salvation—the holy day of Easter—so that we, along with the angels, may celebrate the heavenly Feast.

Remember that Israel, coming out of affliction to a state of rest, sang a song of praise for the victory as they kept the Feast. And in the time of Esther the people kept a feast to the Lord because they had been delivered from a deadly decree (Esth. 3:9; 9:21). They called a feast, thanking and praising the Lord because He had changed the situation for them. Therefore, let us keep our promises to the Lord, confess our sins, and keep the Feast to Him—in behavior, moral conduct, and way of life. Let us keep it by praising the Lord, who has disciplined us so lightly but has never failed us nor forsaken us nor stopped speaking to us.

He has now brought us out of the deceitful and infamous "Egypt" of the enemies of Christ (the Arians). Having experienced many troubles and afflictions in the wilderness, so to speak, we are here with His holy church. From here we can send you the customary Easter Letter, as well as receive letters from you. I'm especially thankful for this privilege, for it is an apostolic custom which these enemies of Christ, and the schismatics along with them, wanted to break off and put an end to. The Lord did not permit it, however, but both renewed and preserved the tradition that He ordained through the apostle Paul. So we may keep the Feast together, and together keep the holy days, according to the tradition and commandment of the Fathers.

THE DATES OF THE EASTER SEASON

We begin the forty-day fast on February 13 and the holy fast of Easter Week on March 20. The fast comes to an end late on the evening of March 25. Then we keep the Feast on the first day of the week, Easter Sunday, March 26. From that day until Pentecost we keep holy day through seven weeks, one after the other. As we set our minds properly on all that this season means, we will be prepared for the eternal realities behind them, through Christ Jesus our Lord, through whom to the Father be glory and dominion forever and ever. Amen.

Greet one another with a holy kiss, remembering us in your holy prayers. All the brothers and sisters who are with me greet you—they keep you in mind all the time. I pray, dear brothers and sisters whom we love more than anything, that you may have health in the Lord.

THE NINTH LETTER

A.D. 339

THE WICKED DIG
A PIT FOR THEMSELVES

INTRODUCTION TO THE NINTH LETTER

Remember that by count we are now two years behind. This is the letter for the eleventh year of Athanasius' ministry as bishop. He was home when he wrote it, but the Arians were stirring up trouble and Athanasius could not complete the fast and celebrate the Feast in peace. On March 19 he had to go into hiding (after baptizing many people in the church of Theonas). He remained quietly in the city through Easter Sunday, but he had to leave for Rome the next day. Although this letter was written in the midst of trials and afflictions, it reflects a mature trust in the Lord and His providence.

This year Athanasius wrote many words about the wicked. They get so involved in lying and evildoing, he says, that they aren't about to repent. But their wickedness comes right back on them. Consider that all those things they throw at others — anger, hatred, bitterness—they already have inside themselves.

He builds a foundation upon which to attack the Arians, whom he calls "Ario-maniacs."[1] His logic here is very strong. There is a close relationship between faith and godliness. The Arians denied the godhead of the Son. That practice undermined their faith and increased their godlessness. Being so godless, they set out to destroy the faith of the simple, spreading their poison everywhere. They really were maniacs! Stay away from them and

[1]This was a common term used for the Arians by the orthodox. They were considered to be madly promoting an insane heresy, and their tactics were known to demonstrate no regard for truth or morality.

their doctrines, he warns. Devote yourself to godliness and keep the true confession of faith.

Athanasius also reminds the people that trouble is coming. The "party of Eusebius," the Arian leadership, are already planning an attack, he warns. Nevertheless, those things aren't worth worrying about. The Lord prophesied afflictions for His people. Therefore, the bishop says, let us keep the Feast with joy.

You know, this connection between faith and godliness is one we should give more attention to. Sometimes Christians look at the apparent good works and the seeming morality of heretics and say, "Aren't they godly?" No, they are not godly! Only those who are in union with Christ are truly godly! "Good works" done with an evil motive are not good, and a morality undertaken in an attempt to be righteous enough to satisfy God is not a godly morality. Only a true and pure faith and godliness from a heart reconciled to God can unite to bear good fruit. Heretics cannot be godly, and wicked men cannot hold the true faith in their hearts.

For as St. Paul says, "The solid foundation of God stands, having this seal: "The Lord knows those who are His," and, "Let everyone who names the name of Christ depart from iniquity" (2 Tim. 2:19).

LETTER IX

A.D. 339

St. Paul, faithful to the Lord and clothed with every godly characteristic (cf. Eph. 6:14) — remember, he did not know of anything in himself which was out of harmony with God's love and purpose (cf. 1 Cor. 4:4)—was so engrossed in holiness that he was carried up to heavenly places. He was taken to Paradise (2 Cor. 12:4), so that even as his way of life was better than that of other people, he might be given an experience higher than theirs.

After he descended from that experience, he preached to all: "We know in part and we prophesy in part . . . here I know in part; but then I shall know just as I am known" (1 Cor. 13:9,12). He truly was already known to the saints in heaven, as their fellow citizen (cf. Eph. 2:19). With respect to those things that are future and perfect, he did know only in part. But with respect to what the Lord had committed and entrusted to him, he was already perfect — as he himself said, "We who are perfect should be thus minded" (Phil. 3:15).

As we know, the gospel of Christ is the fulfillment and realization of the ministry of the Law of Israel. In the same way, future things will be the completion of what presently exists, and the gospel will then be fulfilled. The faithful will receive those things which they do not yet see but hope for, as Paul says, "For who hopes for what he sees? But if we hope for the things we do not see, then we wait patiently for them" (Rom. 8:24,25).

AFFLICTION GIVES WAY TO HAPPINESS

Since that blessed man had such fine character and had the grace of apostleship committed to him, he appropriately wished that everyone should be like him (cf. 1 Cor. 7:7). For godliness is generous, and the kingdom of heaven is very large—a place where thousands of thousands and myriads of myriads serve the Lord.

And although the entrance is "strait and narrow," once inside we see a vast and limitless space, greater than any other anywhere. We have been told of these things by eyewitnesses and heirs. They speak of their trials and distresses: "You have placed afflictions before us" (Ps. 66:11), but then add, "You brought us out into a spacious place" (Ps. 66:12)—and also, "You gave us space in our distress" (Ps. 4:1).

It is a fact, brothers and sisters, that the path of the saints in this life is one full of troubles. They either endure the pain of longing for that which is to come, like the one who said, "Woe is me that I have such a long pilgrimage" (Ps. 120:5, Septuagint) or they are distressed by their longing for the salvation of others, as Paul wrote to the Corinthians, "I'm afraid that when I come to you, God may humble me and cause me to weep and mourn over many who have sinned and not repented of the impurity, fornication and licentiousness which they have practiced" (2 Cor. 12:21). In the same way, Samuel mourned because of the destruction of Saul, and Jeremiah wept because of the captivity of the people of Israel.

Still, after all this affliction and sorrow and mourning, the saints receive divine gladness, pleasure, and exultation when they leave this world. Pain, sorrow, and weeping are left behind.

THE UNIVERSALITY OF ST. PAUL'S TEACHING

With that to look forward to, brothers and sisters, let us never leave the path of godliness. St. Paul urged us to be like him, saying, "Follow me, as I follow Christ" (1 Cor. 11:1). This advice was not meant only for the Corinthians, for since he was "a teacher of the Gentiles in faith and truth" (1 Tim. 2:7), he was not an apostle only to them. Rather, he admonished all of us through them.

In short, all of his various letters to different people contain commands that apply to everybody. He *exhorted* some people, as we see in his letters to the Romans, to the Ephesians, and to Philemon. Some he *reproved*, such as the Corinthians and the Galatians. To some he *gave advice*, as he did to the Colossians and the Thessalonians. He *approved* of the Philippians and indicated that they made him happy. He taught the Hebrews that the Law was a picture to them, a shadow of what was to come.[2] When his chosen sons Timothy and Titus were with him, he taught them; when they were away from him, he reminded them of that teaching.

St. Paul truly was all things to all men. Being mature and godly, he adapted his teaching to the needs of all, so that by all means he might rescue some of them (cf. 1 Cor. 9:22). Therefore, his teaching was not fruitless; rather, it remains planted and productive everywhere, even until now.

And why, dear friends? That's an appropriate question, for we need to understand what the apostle had in mind. He used persuasion and warnings, not only when he opened his letters, but also when he closed them, and even in the middle.

THE ORDER OF RELIGIOUS INSTRUCTION

With the aid of your prayers, I hope to give a true picture of the plans of that holy man. He was very knowledgeable and skilled in these matters of God, and he knew the power of the Lord's teaching. So he deemed it necessary to teach first about Christ and the mystery of His incarnation. Only then did he point to things in their lives that needed to be corrected. He

[2]As was pointed out earlier, St. Athanasius apparently considered St. Paul the author of the Letter to the Hebrews. Though the Pauline authorship is commonly doubted today, the letter was traditionally attached to his writings, and many early Fathers simply accepted him as the author.

wanted them to first know the Lord and then to want to do what He told them. For if you don't know the One who leads His people in observing His commands, you are not very likely to obey them.

Moses, that famous and faithful minister of God, used this method. When he set forth those things having to do with the divine system of laws, he first dealt with the knowledge of God: "Hear, O Israel, the Lord your God is one Lord" (Deut. 6:4). Then, *after* picturing Him to the people, teaching them about the One in whom they should believe, and informing them concerning Him who is truly God—only then did he tell how one can please Him. Only then did he say, "You shall not commit adultery; you shall not steal," and the other commandments.

The reason for this order of teaching is given to us in the apostolic writings: "He who draws near to God must believe that He is and that He is a rewarder of those who seek Him" (Heb. 11:6). He is sought by godly and righteous acts, as the prophet tells us: "Seek the Lord, and when you have found Him, call upon Him; when He is near you, let the wicked forsake his ways and the unrighteous man his thoughts (Isa. 55:6,7).

In the beginning of his book the Shepherd states: "First of all, believe that God is one, who created and completed all things and made all that is from that which is not."[3]

The blessed evangelists, the men who recorded the words of the Lord, each placed at the beginning of his Gospel those things concerning the Savior Himself. They did that so that first having made known the Lord, the Creator, they would be believed when they described the events that took place. Who would have believed their descriptions—of the man who was born blind (and other blind men) recovering sight, of people who rose from the dead, of water turned into wine, or of lepers who were cleansed—if they had not first taught of Him as the Creator, writing as John did, "In the beginning was the Word"

[3]*Shepherd of Hermas*, Mandate I. See Jack Sparks, ed., *The Apostolic Fathers* (Nashville: Thomas Nelson, 1978), p. 183.

(John 1:1)? Or as Matthew wrote, that He who was born of the seed of David was Emmanuel, the Son of the living God? They first presented Him whom the Jews, along with the Arians, reject, but whom we acknowledge and worship.

ST. PAUL'S INSTRUCTIONS TO TIMOTHY

As was proper, the apostle sent instructions to many people, but especially reminded his own son (Timothy) that he should not despise the instruction he had given him (cf. 2 Tim. 3:14). He also commanded him to "Remember Jesus Christ, descended from David and risen from the dead, according to my Gospel" (2 Tim. 2:8).

But he does not just speak of these things so as to remind Timothy of them, but adds, "Meditate on these things and practice them" (1 Tim. 4:15). Constant attention to and meditation upon godly teaching strengthens devotion to God and produces a love for Him which, being deeper than mere words, is actually inseparable from Him. Having that attitude, St. Paul speaks on behalf of himself and others of the same mind, saying boldly, "What shall separate us from the love of God?" (Rom. 8:35). Such people are firmly fixed in the Lord and enjoy an unshakable relationship with Him. As the Scripture says, "He who is joined to the Lord is one spirit with Him" (1 Cor. 6:17).

Thus, they are as solid as Mount Zion, and although they may face ten thousand violent trials, they are founded upon the rock —Christ (1 Cor. 10:4; Matt. 7:25; Ps. 125:1).

THE UNSTABLE CHARACTER OF THE WICKED

The careless, however, do not take any delight in the Lord. Since they do not center their minds on good thoughts, they are dirtied by the daily attacks of sin. Being unfaithful, they value nothing more highly than the things of here and now. For "either the cares of this world, or the deceitfulness of riches, chokes them" (Matt. 13:22). Or, as Jesus put it in the parable that refers to them, they stay with the faith only for a little while because they haven't taken root in it, and then as soon as they face persecution or some problem arises because of the Word, they are offended.

People who cling to evil thoughts do not stand for truth, but for falsehood. They do not stand for righteousness, but for iniquity, because their tongue learns to speak lies. They have done evil, never pausing so that they could repent. Persevering with delight in wicked actions, they run to them without even looking back. They even tread underfoot the commandment about neighbors, and instead of loving them they plot evil against them. As the ancient saint testifies, "Those who plot evil against me have spoken lies and plan treachery all day long" (Ps. 38:12).

But the divine proverb tells us that failure to follow instruction is the cause of such concentration on evil: "The son who forsakes the commandment of his father meditates on evil words" (Prov. 19:27, Septuagint). The Holy Spirit rebukes and reproves this kind of deliberation because it is evil, saying, "Your hands are polluted with blood, your fingers with sins; your lips have spoken lawlessness and your tongue speaks wickedness: none of you tells the truth, nor is there true judgment" (Isa. 59:3,4).

He follows that up immediately by giving the result of such perverse thinking: "They trust in futile things and speak lies; for they conceive mischief and bring forth lawlessness. They have hatched the eggs of an asp and woven a spider's web; he who eats their eggs dies, and when one is crushed a snake is hatched" (Isa. 59:4,5).

He also tells us what hope such people have: "Because righteousness could never reach them, they received darkness when they looked for light; when they waited for brightness, they walked in a thick fog. They shall grope for the wall like the blind, like those who have no eyes; they shall stumble at noonday as if it were midnight; when dead, they shall groan. They shall roar like bears and mourn like doves" (Isa. 59:9–11).

CORRUPTION DESTROYS THE CORRUPT

One thing you can count on: Corruption does not save those

who get into it. On the contrary, it sets itself up against them, tears them down, and brings about their doom. Woe to those people against whom this prophecy is written! For the evil they pursue is sharper than a two-edged sword, and it will first slay those who lay hold of it. Even their own tongue, as the psalmist points out, "is a sharp sword, and their teeth are spears and arrows" (Ps. 57:4).

But the wonderful part is that the one these people plan to harm actually suffers nothing, while they, on the other hand, are pierced by their own spears. That is because inside themselves they have built up anger, wrath, malice, guile, hatred, and bitterness. Although they may not be able to turn these evil thoughts upon others, they find themselves eaten up by their own internal poison. It works out as the psalmist prays, "Let their sword enter into their own heart" (Ps. 37:15). There is also a similar proverb: "The wicked is encircled by the chain of his sins" (Prov. 5:22).

When the Jews plotted together and agreed to treat the Lord unjustly, they forgot that they were bringing wrath upon themselves. Consequently, the Word mourns for them, saying, "Why do they exalt themselves and the nations plot in vain?" (Ps. 2:1). For the schemes of the Jews really were vain when they planned to kill the Life[4] and invented irrational plots against the Word of the Father.

Anyone today who sees how they have been scattered can rightly say, "Woe to them, for they have devised an evil scheme, injuring their own soul by saying, let us bind the righteous man because he is not pleasing to us" (Isa. 3:9,10, Septuagint[5]). That describes them very well, brothers and sisters, for when they purposely misinterpreted the Scriptures they did not know that "he who digs a pit for his neighbor falls in it; and he who tears down a hedge will be bitten by a snake" (Eccl. 10:8).

If they had not turned away from the Lord, they would have

[4]The parallel clause of this sentence shows that "Life" means Christ. Athanasius used the word that way quite often.
[5]Also, Wisdom 2:12.

feared what was written in the divine Psalms: "The heathen are caught in the pit which they made; their own foot is trapped in the snare which they hid. The Lord is known when He executes judgment: the sinner is taken by the work of His hands" (Ps. 9:15,16). Let them take note of this fact and see how "the snare they do not know shall come upon them, and the net they hid shall take them" (Ps. 35:8). But they did not understand these things, for if they had, "they would not have crucified the Lord of glory" (1 Cor. 2:8).

THE RIGHTEOUS ARE DIFFERENT

How different are the righteous and faithful servants of the Lord!

They are "made disciples of the kingdom of heaven and bring forth both new and old things from it" (Matt. 13:52). They "meditate on the words of the Lord when they sit in their houses, when they lie down, when they rise up, and when they walk by the way" (Deut. 6:7). They have a good hope because of the promise of the Spirit, "Blessed is the man who does not walk in the counsel of the ungodly, nor stand in the way of sinners, nor sit in the seat of mockers; but his delight is in the law of the Lord and he meditates on His law day and night" (Ps. 1:1,2).

Being grounded in faith, rejoicing in hope, zealous in spirit, they boldly say, "My mouth shall speak of wisdom, and the meditation of my heart shall be understanding" (Ps. 49:3). And they add, "I meditate on all You have done, and think about the works of Your hands" (Ps. 143:5). And further, "I think of You on my bed and meditate on You in the morning" (Ps. 63:6).

Then, advancing in boldness, they say, "Let the meditation of my heart be acceptable in Your sight" (Ps. 19:14). And what is the reward of such a person? The psalmist adds immediately, "The Lord is my Helper and my Redeemer" (Ps. 19:14).

Nothing *truly bad* can happen to those who examine themselves in this way and bring the desires of their hearts into agreement with the Lord. Indeed, their hearts are strengthened by confidence in the Lord, as it is written, "Those who trust in the Lord shall be as Mount Zion: those who live in Jerusalem shall never be moved" (Ps. 125:1, Septuagint). For if the crafty one should be so bold as to presume to drive a wedge between the saints and divide them, they will look to the Lord not only as their avenger, but if the enemy has already gained an advantage over them, as their deliverer also. We have a promise from God: "The Lord shall fight for you" (Exod. 14:14).

GOD COMFORTS THE RIGHTEOUS

Although the righteous may face persecution and troubles from outside themselves, they will follow the apostle's words and be "steadfast in tribulation and constant in prayer" (Rom. 12:12). By so doing and by keeping their minds on the Lord's commands, they can stand against whatever they have to face. Consequently, pleasing the Lord, they are able to say, "Distress and anguish have come upon me, but Your commandments are my guide" (Ps. 119:143). And since people do good not only in action but also in thought, the righteous one adds, "I awaken before dawn so that I can think about Your promises" (Ps. 119:148).

It is quite proper for those who have been made whole to think about good even before they do it. Our Savior, in His instructions about virtue, begins with the mind, saying, "Whoever looks on a woman to lust for her, has already committed adultery" (Matt. 5:28). And, "Whoever is angry with his brother is guilty of murder" (Matt. 5:22). After all, murder doesn't happen if no anger is built up, and if the mind is clear of lust there will be no adultery.

It follows then that meditation on God's commands and continual occupation with good things are both necessary so "that the saint may be complete, prepared for every good work" (2 Tim. 3:17). Paul, in the passage in which he called such constant contemplation "exercise," told Timothy that it leads to the promise of eternal life: "Exercise yourself in godliness; while bodily exercise is of little profit, godliness is valuable in all ways, since it holds promise not only for the present life but also for that which is eternal" (1 Tim. 4:7,8).

Now there is a man whose holiness is worth admiring, brothers and sisters! Through Timothy he points out to all of us the need to devote our minds to godliness in preference to everything else, and above all to set our minds upon faith in God.

THE WICKED: CORRUPT IN THOUGHT AND DEED

But what grace can the unrighteous person expect even if he thinks he keeps commandments? In actual fact, such a person can't keep even part of the law because his actions will betray what is inside. As the Spirit said, "The fool has said in his heart, there is no God" (Ps. 14:1). This statement is directly followed by one pointing out that their actions correspond with their thoughts: "They are corrupt, and their behavior is evil." The unrighteous person, then, corrupts his body in every possible way: stealing, committing adultery, cursing, getting drunk, and doing similar things.

The prophet Jeremiah condemns Israel for these very crimes, crying out, "Oh, that I had a lodge far off in the wilderness! Then I would leave my people and go there: for they are all adulterers, a body of treacherous people. They bend their tongue like a bow: falsehood has prevailed over truth in the land and they go from one evil to another. But they do not know Me" (Jer. 9:2). Thus, because of their wickedness and lying— and also because of their wicked deeds in running from evil to evil — he rebukes their schemes. But the reason he charges them with unrighteousness is because they did not know the Lord and they were a faithless people.

FAITH AND GODLINESS

Faith and godliness, you see, are so closely allied that they can be considered sisters. Anyone who believes in the Lord is godly, and the person who is godly believes all the more [cf. John 7:17]. Contrariwise, one who is in a state of wickedness will certainly wander from the faith, and one who falls from godliness falls from the true faith. Paul, recognizing this, advised his disciples: "Avoid profane conversations, for they lead people further into ungodliness and their talk eats away like gangrene. And Hymenaeus and Philetus are examples" (2 Tim. 2:16,17). Then he tells what their wickedness was: "They have left the faith, saying that the resurrection is already past" (2 Tim. 2:18).

In another place the apostle says, "And all those who will live godly lives in Christ Jesus will suffer persecution" (2 Tim. 3:12). Then, to help prevent people from renouncing godliness when they are persecuted, he urges them to cling to the faith, "You, therefore, continue in the things you have learned and been assured of" (2 Tim. 3:14). Just as brothers become strongly knit together when one helps another, so faith and godliness, coming from the same family, hang together. A person who gives his attention to one of the two is strengthened by the other. Consequently, wishing Timothy to live godly to the end and to fight the battle in faith, St. Paul says, "Fight the good fight of faith, and lay hold on eternal life" (1 Tim. 6:12).

Anyone who turns away from the wickedness of idols and properly confesses the true God will fight his enemies by faith. We have been speaking of *faith* and *godliness*. Both of them have the same hope: everlasting life. The apostle says, "Fight the good fight of faith, and lay hold on eternal life" and "Exercise yourself in godliness, for it has the promise of the present life and of that which is to come" (1 Tim. 4:7,8).

THE ERRONEOUS DOCTRINES OF THE ARIANS

That is why the Ario-maniacs,[6] being enemies of Christ, have left the church. They have dug a pit of unbelief into which they themselves have fallen. Having grown in their ungodliness, they wreck the faith of simple people [cf. Rom16:18] by blaspheming the Son, saying that He is a creature, made out of nothing. The apostle Paul's words against Philetus and

[6]Athanasius called the Arians "Ario-maniacs" often—and not flippantly, either. He considered them actually to have gone insane with their heresy.

Hymenaeus stand as a warning against ungodliness such as that of the Arians: "God's foundation is firm, bearing this seed: 'The Lord knows His own people' and 'Let everyone who names the name of the Lord depart from iniquity' " (2 Tim. 2:19).

Anyone who hopes to properly celebrate the Feast should stay away from the wickedness and evil deeds being done by sinners, for a person who is splattered by the filth of the wicked is not ready to sacrifice the Passover to the Lord our God. The people of Israel recognized that when they were still in Egypt, so they said, "We cannot sacrifice the Passover to the Lord our God in Egypt" (Exod. 8:26). God, who is over all, wanted them to go far away from the servants of Pharaoh and from the "furnace of iron" (cf. Deut. 4:20; 1 Kings 8:51). He wanted them set free from wickedness and cleansed of all foreign ideas so that they would be able to take in the knowledge of God and of righteous living.

It is as He said through St. Paul, "Come out from among them and be separate from them and do not touch unclean things" (2 Cor. 6:17). For no one is going to turn away from sin and start behaving righteously unless he thinks about what he is doing. Not until he has been straightened out by practicing godly behavior will he actually possess the reward of faith: the crown of righteousness that Paul possessed, having fought the good fight. That crown is laid up not just for Paul, but for all who are like him in this respect.

CHRISTIANS EVERYWHERE UNITED IN SPIRIT

This sort of meditation and exercise in godliness should be familiar to us, as it was to the saints of old. It should be especially so in the season when the divine Word calls upon us to keep the Feast. For what, after all, is the Feast but continual worship of God, recognition of godliness, and unceasing prayer all done from the heart in full agreement with each other? St. Paul, wanting us to be so inclined, urges us, "Always rejoice, pray without ceasing, give thanks in all things" (1 Thess. 5:16–18).

So let us keep the Feast *together*—not with division between us, but unitedly and collectively, as the prophet exhorts: "O come let us rejoice in the Lord; let us make a joyful noise to God our Savior" (Ps. 95:1). Who, then, is going to be so negligent or so disobedient to the divine command that he will not forsake everything and hurry to assemble with the faithful for the Feast? And that Feast, remember, is not held in just one place. It is not just the believers in one location who keep it, for "into all the earth their song has gone forth, and their words have gone to the ends of the world" (Ps. 19:4). The sacrifice is not just offered in one place, but "in every nation incense and a pure sacrifice are offered to God" (Mal. 1:11).

When praise and prayer ascend to our gracious and good Father with such unity from people everywhere; when the catholic church everywhere celebrates together in the same worship to God with gladness and rejoicing; when all the faithful in common send up a song of praise and shout, "Amen!"; that will be such a blessed time, brothers and sisters. Who will not be praying devoutly at that time? The walls of every antagonistic power will fall like those of Jericho, and the gift of the Holy Spirit will be richly poured out upon all [cf. John 7:39; Rom. 5:5; John 20:22]. Then each of us, recognizing the presence of the Spirit, will say, "We are all filled with your grace in the morning, and we rejoice and are made glad all day long" (Ps. 90:14, Septuagint).

THE PARTY OF EUSEBIUS

Therefore, let us make a joyful noise with the saints, and let us all take part as we should, forgetting the afflictions and difficulties that the party of Eusebius is presently causing us.[7] Even now they are plotting against us, hoping to cause our death.

Nevermind: The defender of godliness is the Lord. We are

[7]The Arian heretics were led by Eusebius of Nicomedia. At this very time they were meeting with the emperor, Constantius, to discuss having Athanasius removed as bishop of Alexandria and placing a heretic of their choice in the office. During Lent the persecutors came, and Athanasius had to go into hiding.

faithful servants of His and we know that He will save us when trouble comes. Remember what He promised: "Blessed are you when men revile you and persecute you and say all kinds of evil things about you falsely because of Me. Rejoice and be very glad, for your reward in heaven is great" (Matt. 5:11,12).

Our Redeemer did not say that everybody in this world would have troubles—only those who live in reverence of Him. Therefore, the more our enemies attack us, the more relieved we should be. When they abuse us, we should fight for the faith. And the more they try to turn us away from godliness, the more we should preach it boldly, saying to the Lord, "All these things have come upon us, but we have not forgotten You" (Ps. 44:17). And, "We have not behaved evilly as have the Ario-maniacs who say that You came into being out of nothing." Oh, no, for we know that the Word, who is eternally with the Father, is also from and of His nature.

Therefore, brothers and sisters, let us keep the Feast—and not as a time of grief and mourning. Nor should we let the difficulties we face because of the faith cause us to give up and mingle with heretics. Instead, let us pay attention to those things that promote gladness and joy, lest our hearts become sad like Cain's. Like good and faithful servants of the Lord, we want to hear Him say, "Enter into the joy of your Lord" (Matt. 25:21). These days of Easter are not a time of sorrow and mourning, as some people may think. We come to the Feast full of joy and gladness.

ARIANS, JEWS OPPOSED TO CHRIST

Therefore, we do not keep the Feast in the manner of the deceitful error of the Jews. Nor do we keep it according to the teaching of the Arians, which removes the Son from the Godhead, considering Him a created being. No, we keep the Feast according to the correct doctrine we received from the Lord.

The deceptive error followed by the Jews and the unqualified irreverence of the Arians both lead, finally, only to sad memories. The Jews slew the Lord, and the Arians would remove His conquest of that death, for they say He is not the Creator, but a creature. You see, if He were a creature, death would have held Him. But if as the Scriptures positively state, He was not held by death, then He is no creature but the Lord of creatures — and the substance of this immortal Feast (cf. 1 Cor. 5:7).

For the Lord over death set out to abolish death, and being Lord, He accomplished His aim. Thus we have passed from death to life. But the concept the Jews and those who think like them held about the Lord was all wrong. Things did not turn out at all according to their expectations, for the reverse was true. In fact, "He who sits in heaven shall laugh at them: the Lord shall have them in derision" (Ps. 2:4).

That is why our Savior restrained the women with Him from weeping when He was being led to death: "Weep not for Me" (Luke 23:28). He wished to show that His death was not an event for us to mourn about, but rather to be joyful about, since He who died for us is alive! For He was not created out of nothing; He derives His being from the Father.

PARTAKE OF CHRIST AS TRUE FOOD

It truly is a matter of joy that in the body of the Lord we see the signs of victory over death—our immortality. For since He rose victoriously, so will we; and since His body passed beyond mortality, there can be no doubt about our immortality.[8] The apostle Paul said (and he was telling the truth) that just as through one man [Adam] sin passed to all of humanity, through the resurrection of our Lord Jesus Christ, we shall all rise (Rom. 5:12,18). As he put it in another place, "this perishable nature will put on the imperishable and this mortal will put on immortality" (1 Cor. 15:53).

All of this was accomplished in our Lord's Passion, when He died for us, for "Christ our Passover is sacrificed" (1 Cor. 5:7). Therefore, since He has been sacrificed for us, let us feed upon

[8]See St. Athanasius, *On the Incarnation*, (Crestwood, N.Y.: St. Vladimir's Press, 1977), para. 50, pp. 88–89.

Him, partaking of His nourishment with eagerness and zeal. For He is given to all of us without grudging, and in each of us He is a "well of water flowing to eternal life" (John 4:14).

THE DATES OF THE EASTER SEASON

On March 5 we begin the forty-day fast, purifying ourselves and serving the Lord in abstinence. We commence the activities of Easter Week on April 9, extending the fast until Saturday evening. Then, when the light of the morning dawns upon us on Easter Sunday (April 15), we will already be bright with the light of the Lord.

It is fitting, then, for us to rejoice and be glad—with the joy that springs from good works—for the whole seven weeks from then until Pentecost. And every day we should be giving glory to the Father, saying, "This is the day which the Lord has made: we will rejoice and be glad in it" (Ps. 118:24)—through our Lord and Savior Jesus Christ, through whom to the same and to His Father be glory and dominion forever and ever. Amen.

Greet one another with a holy kiss. All the brothers and sisters who are with me greet you. I pray, dear brothers and sisters, that you will have health in the Lord.

THE TENTH LETTER

A.D. 341

SUFFERING PREPARES US FOR ETERNAL GLORY

INTRODUCTION TO THE TENTH LETTER

Athanasius was not able to send the usual Easter Letter in 340 because the Arians had a false bishop in Alexandria oppressing the people. There is a short letter to his friend Bishop Serapian of Thumuis, which may have been his notice for that year.[1] However, this letter of 341 was sent from Rome, where he had fled for shelter. That fact and that of the persecution of the church by heretics are duly noted in the letter.

In this Festal Letter, Athanasius uses the existing situation to teach some lessons about trials and tribulations. He points out how the Scriptures teach that our faith is tested and tried so that it can be displayed. That is good not only for the one tested but also for those who are reluctant to face trials, because when they see the results, tribulation will look good rather than bad. The wicked, of course, bent on enjoying themselves to the full till they die, hate trials.

What is needed, Athanasius tells his flock, is an eternal outlook. Keep your eyes fixed on the glory that lies ahead, rather than on these temporary things around us. Since we are heirs of God and joint heirs with Christ, we shouldn't even compare present sufferings with the eternal glory to come. Instead, we should be glad when we are faced with all these trials, because they do good things to us. Let us consider them as means to draw closer to God.

[1]*St. Athanasius: Select Works and Letters*, Vol. 4, *A Select Library of Nicene and Post-Nicene Fathers of the Christian Church*, ed. Philip Schaff and Henry Wace, Second Series (Grand Rapids: Eerdmans, 1971), pp. 538–39.

Today we live in a "soft" time, age, and place. There have been many Christian martyrs in our time, but persecution leading to death is unknown in the United States. We live in a society where religious pluralism and tolerance are highly exalted. We have come to expect that Christians, like every other religious group, can anticipate freedom to follow God as they see Him (or gods as they see them). Consequently, the least little bit of pressure because of the faith causes worry and consternation.

In fact, we are so used to the comfortable and secure life of our day that we unconsciously consider any kind of problem *bad*. When trials come we say, "Why me?" and do everything we can to wiggle out of them, assuming, as the lawless do, that trials are bad for us. Oh, dear modern Christians: Awake, for difficulties are to the end that "the genuineness of your faith, being much more precious than gold that perishes, though it is tested with fire, may be found to praise, honor, and glory at the revelation of Jesus Christ" (1 Peter 1:7).

LETTER X

A.D. 341

Dear brothers and sisters: Even though the Arian enemies of Christ have been oppressing both you and us, I am still able to send you the customary notice of the Feast of our salvation.

God is comforting us in our common faith, so although I am keeping the Feast with the people of God here in Rome, I am also keeping it with you in will and spirit. With you, we send up prayers to God, who has made it possible not only for us to believe in Him, but now also to suffer for His sake (Phil. 1:29). Yes, even though it troubles us a great deal to be so far away from you, He is moving us to write so that at least we can comfort each other and stimulate each other to do good (Heb. 10:24).

PERSECUTION OF THE CHURCH BY HERETICS

We have indeed experienced numerous attacks and much bitter persecution aimed at the church. Heretics, unfamiliar with the faith and corrupt in their thinking, have risen up against the truth and are violently persecuting the church. Some of the brothers and sisters have been whipped, and others have been torn apart on the rack. This ill treatment has become so vicious that it has even spread to the bishops. Nevertheless, it is not appropriate for us to neglect the Feast because of such things. Actually, rather than neglecting its celebration, we should be more determined than ever to remember it.

Unbelievers don't really think about such things as seasons for feasts, for they spend all their time in foolishness and carousing. The feasts they do have are times of grief rather than joy. But since for us the feasts are a regular passage to heaven in the midst of this present life, the seasons mean a great deal to us.

Troubles such as we are going through give opportunity to prove and to improve ourselves. Having through them proven ourselves to be choice and eager servants of Christ, we will be revealed as fellow heirs with the saints. As Job said, "The whole world is a trial to men on the earth" (Job 7:1). Perhaps so, but the troubles, sorrows, and travail we go through test us so that we will each receive the proper reward from God. As He says through the prophet, "I am the Lord, who tries hearts and searches minds in order to give to everyone what his life shows he should have" (Jer. 17:10). Of course, He doesn't first learn about a person when he is tested; He knows everything before it happens. But He is good and does good to mankind, so He rewards everyone according to his works.

Consequently, all will have to exclaim in the end, "The judgment of God is righteous!" As the prophet says in another place, "The Lord tries the righteous and understands thoughts and feelings" (Jer. 20:12).

He also has other reasons for trying and testing us. For one thing, He sometimes tests us so our virtues will be revealed by our reaction—as in the case of Job: "Was I revealed to you for any other reason than that you should be seen righteous?" (Job 40:8,9 [vv. 3,4, Septuagint]). Or sometimes He puts people through a trial so that when they see what their own deeds are like, they will realize where they are heading and will either repent of their wickedness or remain steadfast in the faith, as the case requires.

St. Paul, for example, when faced by trouble, persecution, hunger, and thirst was through it all "a conqueror, through Jesus Christ who loved us" (Rom 8:37). Suffering surely weakened his body, but believing and hoping, he was strong in spirit and his strength was made perfect in weakness (2 Cor. 12:9).

CHRISTIANS TRIED FOR THEIR OWN GOOD

The other saints, having the same confidence in God, gladly accepted the same sort of testing — as Job, for example, who said, "Blessed be the name of the Lord" (Job 1:21). And the psalmist *asked* for testing: "Search me, O Lord, and try me: test my heart and my mind" (Ps. 26:2). When strength is tested and proven, even foolish people are convinced.

These saints, because they saw that the "divine fire" would cleanse them and benefit them, did not shrink back from or get discouraged by the trials they faced. Rather than being hurt by what they went through, they grew and were made better, shining like gold that has been refined in a fire (cf. Mal. 3:3; 1 Peter 1:7). As one who had gone successfully through this sort of thing said, "You have tried my heart; You have visited me at night; You have tested me and found no evil in me; I do not harm others with my mouth" (Ps. 17:3).

Rebels, on the other hand, since all they understand is eating, drinking, and dying, consider trials to be dangerous. They very quickly stumble over them, and then, having an untested and unstable faith, their evil minds run free and they fall into improper behavior (cf. Rom 1:28). Therefore St. Paul urges us to exercise our faith in the face of troubles. Having already come through them victoriously, he said, "Therefore I take pleasure in persecutions and weaknesses" (2 Cor. 12:10). In another place he said, "Exercise yourself in godliness" (1 Tim. 4:7). He knew that those who choose to live godly lives are going to be persecuted, so he wanted his disciples to be aware of the difficulties they would face. Then when the trials and afflictions did come, they would have built up enough strength to handle them easily.

You know yourself that when you've been looking forward to something, even if it's hard, you experience a secret joy when it actually comes.

MARTYRS REFINED BY THEIR SUFFERINGS

This is how the blessed martyrs were so quickly matured in

Christ that they were able to keep their minds on the expected rest rather than the pain and injury their bodies would go through (cf. Col. 1:28). They had already experienced trials and troubles that had brought them a long way toward that attitude of life.

What a contrast to those people who name their estates after themselves (Ps. 49:11), and those who have their minds on hay, wood, and stubble (cf. 1 Cor. 3:12)! These people are aliens to the kingdom of heaven because they are strangers to troubles.

Oh, if they only understood that "tribulation works patience, and patience strength of character, and strong character hope, and hope does not disappoint" (Rom. 5:3–5). Then they would have exercised themselves as Paul did: "I buffet my body and keep it under subjection so that after I've preached to others, I will not be disqualified myself" (1 Cor. 9:27).

They would have gladly borne the afflictions that came along in life if they had listened to the prophetic advice: "It is good for a man to take Your yoke in his youth; let him sit alone and be silent when he has taken it up. Let him turn his cheek to the one who strikes him and accept insults. Because the Lord does not reject forever, for when He afflicts, He is gracious, according to the abundance of His tender mercies" (Lam. 3:27–32).

TEMPORAL AFFLICTIONS AND ETERNAL GLORY

For though enemies rain down wounds, insults, and accusations, they amount to nothing when compared to the tender mercies of God. We will quickly recover from such earthly injuries, for God is always gracious and always pours out His tender mercies on those who please Him. Therefore, dear brothers and sisters, we shouldn't pay attention to the things of time and earth. Rather, we should fix our attention on those things that are eternal.

If trouble comes, there will be an end to it; if insults and persecutions fall upon us, they are nothing in comparison to the hope that is set before us. In fact, all present matters are trifling compared with future matters. The sufferings of these days are not even worth comparing with the hope that is to come (cf. Rom 8:18; 2 Cor. 4:17).

What can be compared with the kingdom of God? What is like eternal life? Or what is all that we could possibly give here compared with what we shall inherit there? For we are "heirs of God and joint heirs with Christ" (Rom 8:17). Therefore, dear friends, we shouldn't even think about troubles and persecutions. Our minds should dwell on the hopes that are laid up for us *because* of the persecutions!

IMITATING THE EXAMPLE OF ISSACHAR

Perhaps the example of the patriarch Issachar, as described in the Scriptures, will help to persuade us: "Issachar desires that which is good, resting between the heritages; and when he saw that the rest was good and the land fertile, he bowed his shoulder to work and became a farmer" (Gen. 49:14).[2]

Burning with divine love like the spouse in the Song of Solomon, Issachar obtained the truth from the holy Scriptures. His mind was not absorbed only with the things of earth, but with both things of the present and things to come. Like a bird just beginning to spread its wings, he had a glimpse of "the rest" which is to come in heaven. Knowing that the earth is beautiful, he formed some idea of how much more beautiful the heavenly country is — since it is always bright and new, never growing old. As the Lord said, the "country" we presently possess is passing away, but the one that is waiting for the saints is immortal.

Now when Issachar the patriarch understood these facts, he

[2]I know of no English version in which the first part of this verse is rendered exactly as Athanasius puts it. It is interesting, however, that the Jerusalem *Targum* paraphrases the verse this way: "And he saw the rest of the world to come, that it was good, and the portion of the land of Israel, that it was pleasant; therefore he inclined his shoulders to work in the law, and his brethren brought gifts unto him."

Athanasius' comment on the passage treats it much that way. He sees Issachar as treating this world as what God had given him for the time being — something to be willingly and cheerfully accepted as a blessing, whatever troubles might be associated with it. But he looked forward to that great heritage to come, and this hope was his mainstay through life.

rejoiced in all the hard work and troubles he had to live with and willingly applied himself to the work at hand. Consequently, he did not fight against those who struck him, nor was he disturbed by insults. In fact, all these things made him like a strong man more and more victorious. Earnestly cultivating his "land," he made a profit from it. Oh yes, the Word scattered the seed, but Issachar watchfully tended it so that it brought forth a hundred times what was put into it.

RIGHTEOUS SUFFERING UNITES US TO GOD

It is therefore appropriate, dear friends, for us to take pride in the troubles (cf. Rom 5:3) that come when enemies attack us. And when we are persecuted we should not be discouraged, but instead we ought to press even more earnestly after "the crown of the high calling in Christ Jesus our Lord" (Phil 3:14). When we are insulted, that should not disturb us. We should simply turn our cheek to the one who attacks us and even bow our shoulders for his blows.

The apostle James tells us that those who love pleasure and hostility are tested "when they are drawn away by their own lusts and enticed" (James 1:14). We, however, are going to suffer for the truth. Well, then, when those who deny the Lord attack us and persecute us, let us, "count it all joy, my brethren, when we encounter various trials and temptations, because we know that the testing of our faith produces inner strength" (James 1:2,3).

Let us rejoice as we keep the Feast, brothers and sisters, for we know that although troubles may come, our salvation is sure. Remember that our Savior did not redeem us by taking the easy way; He abolished death by suffering for us. And He warned us about what was in store by saying, "In the world you will have tribulation" (John 16:33). He didn't tell this for the benefit of everyone — only for those who serve Him faithfully and diligently.

On the other hand, "evildoers and deceivers will get worse and worse, deceiving and being deceived" (2 Tim. 3:13). These ignorant people are like false prophets and interpreters of dreams. Drunk, not with wine but with their own wickedness, they make a pretense of priesthood and exult in the threats they throw at you. Don't believe them. Since we are being tried and tested, let us humble ourselves and refuse to be drawn away by them.

Through Moses, God long ago warned His people to the same effect, saying, "If a prophet or a dreamer rises up among you and offers signs or wonders in an attempt to get you to follow and worship strange gods whom you have not known, do not listen to that prophet or dreamer even if the signs or wonders come true. For the Lord your God is testing you to determine whether you will love the Lord your God with all your heart" (Deut. 13:1–3). Remembering this when we are faced with these testings, we will not separate ourselves from the love of God.

But let us keep the Feast now, dear friends — and not as a day of suffering, but as one of joy in Christ, who feeds us every day. Let us be thinking of the One who was sacrificed at Passover time, for our whole celebration is because Christ our Passover was sacrificed (1 Cor. 5:7). He is the One who once brought His people out of Egypt, and now He has abolished both death and the one who has the power of death — that is, the devil (Heb. 2:14). Even now He is bringing shame upon that evil one and giving aid to those who are distressed and cry out to God day and night (Luke 18:7).

THE DATES OF THE EASTER SEASON

We begin the forty-day fast on March 9 and Holy Week on April 13. Thus, we end our fast on Saturday, April 18, and when Easter Sunday dawns on April 19 we begin the period of feasting which lasts until Pentecost. At all times let us sing praises, calling on Christ, for we have been delivered from our enemies by Christ Jesus our Lord, through whom to the Father be glory and dominion forever and ever. Amen.

Greet one another with a holy kiss. All those who are here with me greet you. I pray, my dear brothers and sisters, that you may have health in the Lord.

THE ELEVENTH LETTER

A.D. 342

CHRIST IS OUR HOLINESS

INTRODUCTION TO THE ELEVENTH LETTER

Athanasius lived in Rome more than three years. Thus he was still there when it came time to write the Festal Letter of 342. Exiled from home, separated by miles and by a sea from his beloved flock, he still managed to get a letter to them.

This letter is designed to lead them to holiness. His method, of course, is to point them to Christ, who is the Way, the Shepherd, the Door, the High Priest—indeed, He is our life. He reminds his readers that it is *God* who came to us. He suffered in His flesh so that He could feed us and give us His saving drink.

Therefore, says Athanasius, we don't come to a feast that is a shadow of the real thing, as the Jews did when they ate the Passover. We come to the Lord, who is Himself the Feast. That is, Christ is the true Passover Lamb. At the Table, although we eat bread and drink wine, we eat His flesh and drink His blood, and we are nourished on His glorified humanity. So let us be holy as He is holy. That way we will conquer death and experience the Holy Spirit, the pledge of the kingdom of heaven.

What a message for us! Today we often have a low view of the Incarnation. Either we downplay Jesus' divinity and unconsciously recognize Him as just a man, or we fail to realize the glorious significance of the fact that the Son of God, the Word, took on real humanity. Consequently, it begins to mean little that through faith we are united to Him in baptism, united to His *resurrected* humanity. As a result, we do not accept as real the nourishment He offers at His Table. Therefore, our lives are barren of holiness, for we have denied their very source.

But come! Let us go up to the Feast in faith. Christ our Passover is indeed sacrificed. Let us keep this Passover with Him in faith and in truth. Then let us live as people made holy by that living connection with the Savior, as people who have received those "great and precious promises, that by these you may be partakers of the divine nature, having escaped the corruption that is in the world through lust" (2 Peter 1:4).

LETTER XI

A.D. 342

The joy of our Feast is always with us, brothers and sisters, and always available for those who wish to celebrate it. For the Word, our Lord Jesus Christ, who is all things to us, is always here. He promised that He would be with us forever, saying, "So, I am with you all the days of the world" (Matt. 28:20).

He is the Shepherd, the High Priest, the Way, the Door, and everything at the same time for us. Further, He has been revealed to us as the Feast, for St. Paul writes, "Christ our Passover is sacrificed" (1 Cor. 5:7). He is the one who was long expected. He brought light to bear on the prayer of the psalmist, "My Joy, deliver me from those who surround me" (Ps. 31:7, Septuagint). Deliverance from wickedness is true rejoicing, a true feast, and it is obtained by totally adopting an upright way of life and centering your mind on reverent obedience to God.

It was by such attitudes and behavior that throughout their lives the saints were like men rejoicing at a feast. One found rest in praying to God, as did the blessed David, who rose at midnight to do so (Ps. 119:62). Another was renowned for his songs of praise, as was Moses, who sang a song of praise for the victory over Pharaoh and his taskmasters (Exod. 15). Others worshiped with constant cheerfulness, like the great Samuel and the blessed Elijah. And now, having come to the end of their perfect way of life on earth, they are keeping the Feast in heaven. There they rejoice in the instruction they once received through symbol; now they understand the truth without types or symbols.

CHRIST: OUR GUIDE TO THE FEAST

But what shall we sprinkle ourselves with now (cf. Exod. 29:21; Num. 8:7) to prepare ourselves to celebrate the Feast? And who will guide us on the way to this festival? No one can do this, my dear friends, except the One whose name you will repeat along with me, our Lord Jesus Christ, who said, "I am the Way" (John 14:6). He is the One of whom St. John wrote that He "takes away the sin of the world" (John 1:29). He is also the One who purifies our souls, as Jeremiah told us, "Stand in the roadway and look for and ask for the path to righteousness, and in it you will find cleansing for your souls" (Jer. 6:16).

In ancient Israel, the blood of male goats and the ashes of a heifer were sprinkled upon those who were considered unclean. But these things were only to purify the body (Heb. 9:13). Now, however, through the grace of God the Word, we are all cleansed inside and out. When we follow Him, we are able even on earth to contemplate the eternal Feast, as if we stood on the very doorstep of the heavenly Jerusalem. Thus the blessed apostles, by unreservedly following their Leader, the Savior, became teachers of that attitude. They simply said, "Behold, we have left everything and followed you" (Mark 10:28).

Of course, following the Lord and keeping His Feast is not just a matter of words; actions are required. Every set of laws and commands involves definite things to be done. For example, when Moses gave the holy laws of God to Israel, he extracted from them a promise to obey—a promise intended to keep them from being labelled liars for neglecting the commands (Exod. 19:8). Therefore, when it came to the celebration of the Feast of the Passover, there was no question to be raised and no reply to be made. When the instructions were given, the Jews obeyed. Moses simply said, "And the children of Israel shall keep the Passover" (Exod. 12:47), expecting that they would obey without question, so that everything would go smoothly.[1]

Well, on such things as this I have confidence in your wisdom and your concern for doctrine. After all, I have dealt with these things often and in several letters.

THE JEWISH PASSOVER: "TYPE" OF THINGS TO COME

Above all, however, I wish to remind you, and myself along with you, that the Lord would not have us come to the Easter Feast irreverently or unprepared. We must have our doctrine straight, follow the proper liturgy, and do all things properly. The historical record of Israel's feast tells us, "No foreigner, no slave purchased with money, no uncircumcised man, may eat the Passover" (Exod. 12:43,44). Nor is it supposed to be eaten in just "any" house; there is a proper place. Also, He commands it to be done in haste, because we were once groaning under the sorrow of our "bondage to Pharaoh" and the "commands of the taskmasters." In the old days, the children of Israel were considered ready to receive the Feast, which was the "type," only if they had followed the instructions. And that type was the forerunner of our Feast, although the Feast was not established *because* of the type.

When the Word of God was ready to establish the Feast, which is the fulfillment of all, He told His disciples, "I have longed very much to eat this Passover with you" (Luke 22:15). The account of how the Passover was to be celebrated, as given to us in the Scriptures (Exod. 12:11–13), presents a marvelous word-picture of what they must have looked like.

Had we been there, we would have seen them equipped like

[1]Athanasius is arguing from Scripture. In Exod. 19:3–7 we read that God gave Moses the terms of the Covenant with Israel. These terms were simple: They were to obey whatever commands God gave them. When Moses told the people, they said (v. 8): "All that the Lord has said we will do." *After that* they were given the Law. The command to keep the Passover was also renewed. So the Israelites had both their promise and their duty of obedience to God as binding reasons to keep it.

people going to a show or a dance. Each carried a staff, wore sandals, and carried unleavened bread. Well, these things done then were shadows and types. But now we have the Truth with us: the "Image of the invisible God" (Col. 1:15), our Lord Jesus Christ, the true Light. Rather than a staff, we have Him for our scepter. Instead of unleavened bread, we have Him — the Bread of Life. He has replaced sandals with the preparation of the gospel (Eph. 6:15). In summary, He has guided us to the Father by all these things.

If enemies attack and persecute us, He will encourage us more than Moses, saying, "Be of good cheer: I have overcome the wicked one" (John 16:33). And if, after we have "passed through the Red Sea," heat oppresses us or we encounter bitter waters, He will come to give us water from His sweet and life-giving fountain. For He says, "If anyone is thirsty, let him come to me and drink" (John 7:37).

CHRIST'S SUFFERINGS—OUR BLESSINGS

Why then do we linger? Why do we delay? Why do we fail to come eagerly and diligently to the Feast, trusting that it is Jesus who calls us? After all, He is all things to us, and He was burdened in ten thousand ways for our salvation. He hungered and thirsted because of us, yet He nourishes us and gives us His saving drink. His glory and the miracle of His divinity is that He exchanged our sufferings for His happiness. Being Life, He died to make us alive. Being the Word, He became flesh so that the flesh might be guided by the Word. Being the fountain of life, He thirsted our thirst in order to call us to come to the Feast, saying, "If anyone is thirsty, let him come to Me and drink" (John 7:37).

In his time, Moses announced the beginning of the Feast by saying, "This month is the beginning of months for you" (Exod. 12:2). But the Lord who came in the fullness of time announced a different day (Heb. 9:26). It was not as if He would abolish the Law given through Moses — far from it. No, He came to establish the Law and, indeed, to fulfill the Law. As St. Paul says, "Christ is the end of the Law to everyone who believes in righteousness" (Rom. 10:4) and "Do we make the Law void by faith? By no means! On the contrary we establish the Law" (Rom. 3:31).

CHRIST: SUM AND SUBSTANCE OF THE PROPHECIES

These things astonished the police officers the Jews sent to arrest Him, so that they reported back to the Pharisees in amazement, "No man ever spoke as this man does" (John 7:46). What was it that astonished and amazed them? Simply the boldness and authority of our Savior. For they knew that the prophetic Scriptures and those who interpreted them always pointed to someone who would come. Moses wrote: "The Lord will raise up a prophet like me from among you. Listen to all that he tells you" (Deut. 18:15). And Isaiah wrote, "Behold, a virgin shall conceive and bear a Son and you shall call his name Emanuel" (Isa. 7:14). Others prophesied about the Lord in a number of different ways.

The Lord, however, prophesied these things not of someone else, but solely of Himself, saying, "If anyone is thirsty, let him come to Me" (John 7:37) — not to any other person, but to "Me." And in those words we hear Him saying, "You may hear about My coming from others. But you must no longer drink from others, but from Me."

Therefore, when we come to the Feast, we must not treat it as the shadows and pictures that Israel had, for they are fulfilled. Nor should we come to it as we would an ordinary secular feast. Oh, no! Let us go quickly to the Lord, who is Himself the Feast (1 Cor. 5:7). We must not look at the Feast as a time to delight the appetite and overindulge, but as a display of virtue.

The feasts of the heathen are made up of laziness and greed. They think idleness is the mark of a feast, and when they feast they do the despicable acts of death and hell. Our feasts, on the other hand, are scenes of virtuous activities and the practice of temperance. The prophetic Word says it very clearly, "The fasts of the fourth, fifth, seventh and tenth months shall become feasts of joy and gladness for the house of Judah" (Zech. 8:19).

CHRISTIANS SHOULD STRIVE FOR HOLINESS

Since this occasion for the exercise of holiness has been established, since the day has come, and since the prophetic voice has called us to the celebration, let us give our full attention to this grand proclamation. Like competitors in a race, let us rival each other in observing the fast in purity; in our attention to prayer; in our study of the Scriptures; in giving to the poor; and in keeping peace with our enemies.

Let us get rid of pride and take on humility, maintaining peace with everyone and urging the brothers and sisters to love. We have before us the example of St. Paul, who often fasted and prayed and was willing to be damned for the sake of his brothers and sisters (Rom. 9:3). Remember how the blessed David first humbled himself by fasting and then went boldly to the Lord: "O Lord my God, if I have done this: if I have done evil with my hands, if I have repaid with evil those who did good to me, then may my enemies overcome me as an ineffectual man" (Ps. 7:3,4,Septuagint).

If we act like these saints of old, we will conquer death and most assuredly receive the promised pledge of the kingdom of heaven.[2]

THE DATES OF THE FEAST

We begin Easter Week on April 5 and end the holy fasts on the evening of Saturday, April 10. Then we keep the holy Feast on the next day, April 11, and add feast days one by one until the holy day of Pentecost. On that day we keep the festival to the Spirit, who is always near us in Jesus Christ, through whom and with whom to the Father be glory and dominion forever and ever. Amen.

[2]The Holy Spirit. See Eph. 1:13,14; 2 Cor. 1:22; 5:5.

THE TWELFTH LETTER

A.D. 347

BE STRONG IN THE FAITH

INTRODUCTION TO THE TWELFTH LETTER

You will note that there is a gap of four years between the last letter and this one. The Festal Letters for 343 and 344 are missing, and those for 345 and 346 are very short, containing only a brief notice of the dates, but no message. During this time a council was held at Sardica (later Sophia in Bulgaria), intended to settle the continued disputes. Athanasius and other exiled bishops were examined and restored.

Nevertheless, the good bishop could not return. It was not until 346 that the Arian Emperor Constantius bowed to truth and allowed him to return to his flock. He had just returned home when he wrote this Festal Letter for 347. Written at the prime of his life (he was forty-eight), it is the letter of a mature man of Christ—a godly bishop—to his flock.

But alas! Although Athanasius was bishop until 373, we have only fragments of the letters that come after this one. I, for one, hope that someday an obscure cache of church documents will reveal the rest in their entirety. What a treasure they will be!

In this, our last letter, Athanasius devotes considerable space to teaching about how the Jews missed the full significance of the Law and the sacrifices, primarily the Passover. Concerning the Law he says, "They conformed to its letter, but they did not submit to its spirit." As a matter of fact, since they treated the whole of God's revelation that way, they don't really have a Passover anymore. They deserted the faith. All this he shows from the Scriptures.

But, he emphasizes, this isn't just a bit of history. These things were written for *our* benefit so that *we* wouldn't suffer shipwreck of the faith. Don't be like unbelievers and turn away when things get tough. Don't let the pleasures of the flesh carry you away. Don't build your house on sand. Turn away from wickedness; give thanks to God; and keep the Feast, looking forward to eternal joy in heaven.

How relevant to us who are Christians today! We are taken by the pleasures of this life, so much so that we see many who are lauded as Christian leaders committing adultery, getting divorces, and being swept away by money and power. They built their houses on sand, they became shipwrecks of the faith, and they are being swept by the current of evil down the swift tunnel to hell. Be not like such people, but repent. "Draw near to God and He will draw near to you. Cleanse your hands, you sinners; and purify your hearts, you double-minded. Lament and mourn and weep! Let your laughter be turned to mourning and your joy to gloom. Humble yourselves in the sight of the Lord, and he will lift you up" (James 4:8–10).

Alas! and Did My Saviour Bleed?

Alas! and did my Savior bleed,
And did my Sov'reign die?
Would He devote that sacred head
For such a worm as I?

Was it for crimes that I had done
He groaned upon the tree?
Amazing pity, grace unknown,
And love beyond degree!

Well might the sun in darkness hide
And shut his glories in
When God, the mighty Maker, died
For man the creature's sin.

Thus might I hide my blushing face
While His dear cross appear,
Dissolve my heart in thankfulness,
And melt mine eyes to tears.

But drops of grief can ne'er repay
The debt of love I owe;
Here, Lord, I give myself away,
'Tis all that I can do.

—Isaac Watts, 1707

LETTER XII

A.D. 347

"Blessed is God, the Father of our Lord Jesus Christ" (Eph. 1:3). What an appropriate introduction for a letter! It fits most especially now, along with the apostle's words of thanksgiving to the Lord.[1] He has brought us back home and given us the privilege of openly sending you the customary Festal Letter.

This is the season of the Feast, brothers and sisters. The day is near and it is not announced with a blast of trumpets, as the Old Testament tells us was done in ancient Israel. No, it is announced and given to us by the Savior, who suffered for us and rose again. As Paul put it, "Christ our Passover is sacrificed" (1 Cor. 5:7).

Therefore, the Feast of the Passover now belongs no longer to the Jews, or to some stranger, but to *us*. For the times of the types and shadows have passed by and the old practices have come to an end. And now the "month of new things" is at hand—the time when everyone should keep the Feast in obedience to Him who said, "Observe the month of new things, and keep the Passover to the Lord your God" (Deut. 16:12, Septuagint).

Even the heathen think they keep festival, and the Jews hypocritically pretend to do so. But He reproves the feast put on by the heathen as food set out for mourners at a funeral. And He turns His face away from the feast of the Jews, for they are

[1]". . . who has blessed us with all spiritual blessings in heavenly things in Christ." Athanasius had been away from home for nearly three years: he was comparing the rest he (and the church) were having from their enemies with the blessings for which the apostle Paul thanked God.

now outcasts. He says to them, "My soul hates your new moons and your sabbaths" (Isa. 1:14).

Actions carried out contrary to the will of God or without proper reverence don't do any good, no matter what religious importance people place on them. As a matter of fact, they are actually an indication of hypocrisy on the part of those who do them. Such people may think they are offering sacrifices to God. But He tells them: "Your whole burnt-offerings are not acceptable and your sacrifices do not please Me; and although you bring fine flour, it is useless; I also abhor your incense" (cf. Isa. 1:13; Jer. 6:20).

God doesn't need anything! And since nothing can make Him unclean, He has had His fill of their hypocritical activities. As He says through Isaiah, "I have had enough" (Isa. 1:11).

THE BLINDNESS OF THE JEWS

There was a law given about these things, and its purpose was to instruct the people and to give a picture of what was to come. As St. Paul puts it in his letter to the Galatians, "Before faith came, we were kept guarded under the Law, kept in custody for the faith which was to come; therefore the Law was our guide to Christ, so that we could be justified by faith" (Gal. 3:23,24).

But the Jews did not grasp or understand that, so they walked in the daytime as if it were darkest night. They felt for the truth which we know to be embedded in the Law, but they never even touched it. Oh, they conformed to its letter, but they did not submit to its spirit. When Moses was veiled, they looked at him, but when he uncovered his face they looked away (Exod. 34:33–35). They did not know what they read, and erroneously substituted one thing for another (cf. 2 Cor. 3:12–18).[2]

HOW THE SCRIPTURES REPROVED THE JEWS

That is why the prophet cried out against them (cf. Isa. 57:4).

[2]Athanasius was pointing out that despite the fact that the Jews misinterpreted the Law, it was intended to lead them to faith in the Son.

The Lord also said of them, "The strange children have dealt falsely with me; the strange children have wilted" (Ps. 18:45 Septuagint). Still, look how gently He reproved them, "Had you believed Moses, you would have believed Me, for he wrote about Me" (John 5:46).

But because they did not believe, they went on to deal falsely with the Law — interpreting things the way they wanted them rather than understanding the Scripture. They also hypocritically distorted the plain text of Scripture. And since they put their confidence in these distortions and misinterpretations, He is angry with them, as shown in Isaiah, "Who wants these things from you?" (Isa. 1:12). And since they were so brazen about it, He threatens them through Jeremiah, "Gather up your whole burnt-offerings and your sacrifices and eat them; for when I brought your fathers out of Egypt, My commands were not given for the sake of the offerings and sacrifices" (Jer. 7:21, 22).

The Jews, you see, did not behave as they should, nor was their observance of the Law carried out with the proper attitude. As the prophet accuses, they were out to serve their own pleasure on their feast days. They oppressed their servants and gathered themselves together for fighting and quarreling. They also beat down the poor, and did everything possible to promote their own gratification.

So you see how it happens that from now to the end of time they will have no feast, even though they make a big display of eating a lamb — in the wrong place and at the wrong time. Instead of sacrificing the lamb in the manner required by God, they have learned to sacrifice to Baal. And instead of accepting the true unleavened Bread, "the children gather wood and their fathers kindle the fire and the women prepare the dough to make cakes for the queen of heaven. And they pour out drink offerings to strange gods in order to make Me angry, says the Lord" (Jer. 7:18).

They have received what they deserve for such deceptions, for although they pretend to keep the Passover, they are unable to express joy and gladness. As Jeremiah put it, "The voice of those who rejoice and are glad — the voice of the bridegroom and the bride — has been taken away from the cities of Judah and the streets of Jerusalem" (Jer. 7:34). Consequently, "he among them who sacrifices an ox is like the one who kills a man; and he who sacrifices a lamb is like a man who kills a dog; he who offers fine flour is like one who offers swine's blood; and he who makes a memorial offering of frankincense is like a blasphemer" (Isa. 66:3). These sacrifices and offerings will never please God, nor has the divine Word required them.

What He *has* said is, "These people have chosen to go their own ways; and their soul delights in their abominations" (Isa. 66:3). What does this mean, brothers and sisters? We need to investigate what the prophet is saying, especially in regard to heretics who think up things contrary to the Law.

THE LAW CONCERNING SACRIFICES

Through Moses God gave commandments about sacrifices, and the whole book of Leviticus is taken up with acceptable ways for them to be carried out. The Lord, through the prophets, found fault with those who contemptuously mistreated these things, calling them disobedient to the commandment. He told them, "I have not asked you to do these things! . . . Neither did I speak to your fathers about sacrifices, nor give them commands about whole burnt-offerings" (Isa. 1:12; Jer. 7:22).

Some have put forth the opinion that either the Scriptures do not agree or that God, who gave the commandment, is a liar. But there is no disagreement—far from it. The Father, who is truth, cannot lie, "for it is impossible for God to lie" (Heb. 6:18), as Paul affirms.[3] Actually, these things are plain to those who accept the writings of the Law with faith and look at them in the right way.

Here is my explanation, and may God grant by your prayers that I'm not too far from the truth. It does not appear to me that God gave the commandments and the Law concerning sacrifices right away when He led them out of Egypt. Nor did He who

[3]Again, the quote from Hebrews is attributed to St. Paul, as if Athanasius accepted Pauline authorship.

gave the Law really pay any attention to the whole burnt-offerings, as such. He was looking ahead to those things that were prefigured and pointed out by them: "For the law contained a shadow of good things to come" (Heb. 10:1). And, "Those regulations were set forth until the time of reformation" (Heb. 9:10).

That is why the whole Law didn't deal with sacrifices, although it did include commands concerning them. By means of these commands it began to teach people, calling them away from idols and drawing them to God, giving them proper teaching for the times in which they lived. So you see, God did not give the people those commands about sacrifices and offerings when He brought them out of Egypt, nor even when they first came to Mount Sinai. God is not like people, that He should want those things for Himself. No, He gave the commandment so that they might know Him and His Word (the Son) — and forget about those so-called gods that don't really exist but appear to do so because of the show people put on.

Notice that He made Himself known to them by bringing them out of the land of Egypt, right through the Red Sea. But then they wanted to serve Baal and dared to offer sacrifices to gods that do not exist. They forgot the miracles that were done for them in Egypt and even thought about going back there again (cf. Exod. 16:3).

After that, indeed *after* the Law had been given, God gave them the commandments dealing with sacrifices. He did this so that their minds, which had once been devoted to those nonexistent gods, could be turned toward Him who really is God. Then they would learn, not especially to sacrifice, but most of all to turn away from idols and to pay attention to God's commands. For after He says, "I have not told you to make sacrifices nor given you commands about whole burnt-offerings" (Jer. 7:22), He immediately adds, "But this is what I commanded them: obey Me and I will be your God and you will be My people and you shall do all that I command you" (Jer. 7:23).

He had already instructed them not to serve anyone but the Lord. They were able to know how long the types and shadows would last. They had been taught not to forget that the time was coming when the sacrifice would no longer be the bullock of the herd, nor the ram of the flock, nor the he-goat (Exod. 12:5).

Further, they knew that all these things should be carried out in a pure and spiritual manner—with constant prayer, a righteous way of life, and godly speech. As David sings, "May my meditation be pleasing to Him. . . . Let my prayer come before you as incense, and the lifting up of my hands as the evening sacrifice" (Ps. 104:34; 141:2). And the Holy Spirit, who was in David, commanded, "Offer to God the sacrifice of praise, and pay your vows to the Lord. . . . Offer the sacrifice of righteousness and put your trust in the Lord" (Ps. 50:14; 4:5).

THE OBSTINACY OF THE JEWS

The great Samuel once very pointedly reproved Saul by saying, "Is not the word better than a gift?" (cf. 1 Sam. 15:22[4]). It is by obedience and praise that one fulfills the Law and pleases God. As He says, "You glorify Me when you bring a sacrifice of praise" (Ps. 50:23). He wants us to "learn the meaning of this: I want mercy and not sacrifice" (Hos. 6:6; Matt. 9:13) and not to condemn our enemies.

But this displeased the Jews. Obviously, they were not eager to understand, "for had they known, they would not have crucified the Lord of glory" (1 Cor. 2:8). The prophet foretold their doom with his words, "Woe to them! For they have thought up an evil plan, saying, let us ambush the righteous man because he is an inconvenience to us" (cf. Isa. 3:9,10[5]). Giving themselves over to evil in this way could only result in heresy, as the Lord said when He reproved them: "You are wrong because you do not know the Scriptures" (Matt. 22:29).

Later, when the reproof they had received should have brought them to their senses, they grew insolent instead and announced, "We are the disciples of Moses and we know that God spoke to him" (John 9:28,29). By saying those things they not only went deeper into deception and false dealings, but

[4]Also, Ecclus. 18:17.
[5]Also, Wisdom 2:12.

they also accused themselves. For if they had actually believed Moses, they would not have denied the Lord, who spoke through Moses, and who was now actually right there with them.

Certainly the eunuch described in Acts was not like them. When he heard, "Do you understand what you read?" (Acts 8:30) he was not ashamed to confess his ignorance. Indeed, he asked to be taught, and because he wanted to learn he was given the grace of the Spirit.

But as for the Jews, because they persisted in their sins the proverb applies to them. "Death came upon them. For the fool dies in his sins" (cf. Prov. 5:23; Prov. 24:9, Septuagint; Ps. 55:15). The same is true for the heretics, who have lost true discernment and dare to believe in atheism. "For the fool says in his heart, there is no God. They are corrupt and they commit foul and wicked acts" (Ps. 14:1). Count on it: those who are fools in their thoughts will do wicked deeds. As the Lord said (to the Pharisees), "How can you speak good things when you are evil?" (Matt. 12:34). And they truly were evil, because their thoughts were wicked.

Or consider, how can a person whose mind is set on fraud act justly? Or how can a person love who has made up his mind to hate? How can someone who is bent upon the love of money be kind? How can a man who deliberately lusts after a woman be pure? "For out of the heart came evil thoughts, fornication, adultery, murder" (Matt. 15:19).

A fool is wrecked by these things like a helpless ship tossed by waves, for all of those bodily pleasures he delights in entice him and drag him under. As it is written, "A fool's whole flesh is tempest-tossed" (Prov. 26:10, Septuagint). So he first gets into foolishness, then is caught in a tempest, and finally perishes, as Solomon says in the Proverbs, "The fool and the person who lacks understanding will perish together, and will leave their wealth to strangers."[6]

Now the Jews suffer these things because not one of them has

[6]The statement is not found in Proverbs but in Ps. 49:10. Athanasius got his reference mixed.

a sound enough mind to guide them. Where there is good judgment, the Word (the Son), who is the pilot of souls, guides the vessel. "For he who has understanding shall possess guidance" (Prov. 1:5), but those who are without guidance fall like the leaves.

THE DISCIPLES CONTINUED STEADFAST

Some fall away completely like Hymenaus and Philetus, who held evil opinions about the Resurrection and consequently suffered shipwreck in the faith. Judas, the betrayer, fell away from the Pilot and perished with the Jews. But the other disciples were wise and stayed with the Lord. And when the sea was agitated and the sky was splashed by waves because of a storm and a contrary wind, they did not fall away. Rather, they awoke the Word, who was sailing with them. At His command the sea became smooth, and they were saved (Mark 4:35–41).

They later became preachers and teachers, telling the stories of the miracles of our Savior and teaching us to follow their example. What they wrote is for us and for our benefit, so that through a knowledge of His signs and wonders we may come to know the Lord who performed them. Therefore, let us maintain the faith of the disciples and live in close relationship with our Master.

THE WORLD COMPARED WITH THE SEA

Brothers and sisters, to us the world is like the sea, of which it is written, "There is the great and wide sea; there go the ships and the Leviathan which you have created to play in it" (Ps. 104:25,26). On this sea we float along, carried by our own free will, as if by the wind. Everyone sets his course according to his will: either he enters into rest with the Word (the Son) as his Pilot, or he falls for the pursuit of pleasure and runs into perilous storms and gets shipwrecked.

Just as there are windstorms and rain out in the ocean, so there are many troubles and trials in the world. Someone who really doesn't believe "stumbles when affliction or persecution arises" (Mark 4:17). Having his eyes on temporal things and not being firmly fixed in the faith, he cannot bear up under the difficulties that result from afflictions. He is like the house built on sand (Luke 6:49) by the foolish man. Since he doesn't understand what is going on, he falls when the winds of temptation blow on him.

The saints, however, do not wither in the face of trials. Their ability to discern has been trained by practice (Heb. 5:14), and they understand the Word and are strong in faith. Although the trials may sometimes be greater as time goes on, they remain faithful. "Awakening" the Lord, who is with them, they are delivered.

So "passing through fire and water" to a place where they can breathe freely, they keep the Feast properly, giving praise and thanksgiving to God, who has redeemed them. Having been tempted, they are known by God, as Abraham was. Or having suffered, they are approved by Him, as was Job. Or being oppressed and deceitfully treated, they patiently endure it like Joseph. Or being persecuted, they are not conquered. Rather, as it is written, they "leap over the wall" (Ps. 18:29) of wickedness that divides and separates brothers, turning them from truth.

In this manner St. Paul rejoiced, taking pleasure in his infirmities, in disgrace, in need, in persecution, and in distress for Christ. In fact, he wanted all of us to rejoice, for he said, "Rejoice always; in everything give thanks" (1 Thess. 5:18).

THE PROPER OBSERVANCE OF THE FEAST

What is more in harmony with the Feast than turning from wickedness to pure behavior, unceasing prayer, and thanksgiving to God? While looking forward to the celebration of eternal joy in heaven, let us keep the Feast here as well—rejoicing at all times, constantly praying, and giving thanks to the Lord in everything. I, for one, give thanks to God that even though He has severely disciplined us, He has not delivered us over to death. Indeed, He brought us back from a long way off, sometimes seeming like the ends of the earth, to unite us with you once again. And yes, I thank Him for all the various ways He has helped us, as well as for the many wonders He has done.

As I have prepared to keep the fast myself, I have also been eager to give you notice of it and of the great Feast of Passover (Easter). For I want very much for us to go up together, as it were, to Jerusalem, and eat the Passover with no division between us, but as people in one house. Yes, and let us divide the Word of God, not watered down as if boiled in water; nor let us disobey the commands of the gospel, having "broken its bones." Rather, let us keep the Feast with penitence and thanksgiving, "roasted with fire, with bitter herbs" — that is, prostrating ourselves before God in fasting and prayer, maintaining an earnest and sincere attitude (Exod. 12:8,9,46).[7]

THE DATES OF THE FAST AND FEAST

We begin the forty-day fast on the second day of March. Then, after we have properly fasted and prayed through that period, we will be prepared for the holy day. Anyone who treats the fast of forty days lightly, rashly, and impurely treads holy things underfoot and cannot celebrate the Easter festival. Let us call each other to remembrance and stimulate one another not to be forgetful or fail to fast on those days. Then the fasts will point us to our goal and we will bring the Feast to a close in the appropriate manner.

As we said, then, the forty-day fast begins on March 2. The great week of the Passover begins on April 6. Let us rest from the fast late in the evening of Saturday, April 11. Let us keep

[7]The play on words refers to how the flesh of the Paschal lamb was to be prepared. If it were boiled, water would be mixed with it. The application is that we are to know nothing but Jesus Christ crucified (1 Cor. 2:2). Further, just as the bones of the Paschal lamb were not to be broken, we are not to disobey the commands of God.

The Passover was to be eaten in one house. Therefore, we are to celebrate the Christian festival with unity of spirit. We are not to be schismatics, but rather we are to be as one house—the one, holy, catholic, and apostolic church. As the Paschal lamb was to be roasted with fire, we also are to burn like a flame in our zeal for the Lord. The bitter herbs remind us to watch and pray to bring forth fruits of repentance.

the Feast, therefore, on Sunday, April 12. And then let us add, one after the other, the seven holy weeks of the feast from Easter to Pentecost Sunday. During the whole of that time, let us rejoice and praise God. For it is He who has given us these special times every year to tell us of the joy and everlasting rest that is prepared in heaven for those of us who truly believe in Christ Jesus our Lord—through whom and with whom be glory and dominion to the Father, with the Holy Spirit, forever and ever. Amen.

Greet one another with a holy kiss. The brothers and sisters who are with me greet you.[8]

[8]To this letter Athanasius added a list of changes in bishops in the area for which he was responsible.

PART III

OUR RESPONSE

LET *US* CELEBRATE THE FEAST

We have come to a time in which we, the people of the church, tend to see Eastertime only as a remembrance of a set of historical events. But when we fail to go beyond remembering, we lose much of Easter's significance. We need the sense of participation in our redemption, of "being there"; of feeling the doom of death and the life of resurrection.

But this does not come by merely thinking about these things. Human experience can never be fulfilled in the mind alone. The fast is part of the participation of the body, and the body is indeed part of us. We are each a unity: body, soul, heart, mind, will, spirit — all bound into one person. Thus, when we fast the body *feels* it and participates in the reason for which we fast.

Understand, then, that a fast is not just a formal abstinence from food for a certain period, nor is it an abstinence to gain points with God. It is a discipline exerted upon ourselves. The great fourth-century preacher John Chrysostom made pointed reference to total participation in a sermon on fasting:

> Do you fast? Give me proof of it by what you do! What do I mean? Well, if you see a poor man, take pity on him! If you see a beautiful woman, don't dwell on fornication! Don't fast by the mouth, but also the eye, the ear, the feet, the hands — all members of your body. Let your hands fast by being pure from stealing and taking things which others should have. Let your feet fast by not running to watch things you shouldn't. Let your eyes fast, being taught not to look at things they shouldn't, and

> especially not to stare at beautiful women. . . . Let the ear fast also. The fasting of the ear consists in refusing to listen to evil talk and rumors. . . . Let the mouth, too, fast from disgraceful talk.[1]

Obviously, John had preparation in mind. To him, it would be silly to abstain from food just to abstain from food. In the same sermon he said:

> . . . when Lent makes its appearance, like a kind of spiritual summer, let us as soldiers burnish our weapons; and as farmers let us sharpen our sickles; and as sailors let us order our thoughts against the waves of extravagant desires; and as travellers let us set out on the journey towards heaven; and as wrestlers let us strip for the contest.[2]

That's what we need to do in preparing for the Great Feast, the Great Eucharist—Easter. Let *us* subdue our bodies and put evil thoughts out of our minds and prepare ourselves to celebrate our redemption. Let *us* in the church in this twentieth century attend to the Scripture readings in the weeks before Easter. Let *us* prepare our hearts with pure thoughts and prayers. We read in a preserved fragment of Athanasius' Letter for 348:

> In these days of the Passover, we should rise early with the saints and come to the Lord with all our soul, with purity of body, with confession and godly faith in Him. Thus, when we have drunk and been filled by the divine water which flows from Him, we will be prepared to sit at table with the saints in heaven, and to share with them in their one voice of joy and gladness.

Then, when the day of resurrection dawns, let the church gather with hopeful, thankful hearts, and let us keep the Feast with our Lord, for Christ our Passover is sacrificed for us, and He said:

[1]Paraphrased from *Sermons of John Chrysostom*, Vol. 9, *A Select Library of the Nicene and Post-Nicene Fathers*, ed. Philip Schaff, trans. W.R.W. Stephens, First Series (Grand Rapids: Eerdmans, 1956).
[2]*Ibid.*

Whoever eats My flesh and drinks My blood has eternal life, and I will raise him up at the last day. For My flesh is food indeed, and My blood is drink indeed. He who eats My flesh and drinks My blood dwells in Me, and I in him As the living Father sent Me, and I live because of the Father, so he who feeds on me will live because of Me (John 6:54–57).

SUGGESTED READINGS FOR THE FORTY FAST DAYS OF LENT

Day	
1	Psalm 68 and "Life of Athanasius" (Chapter Two)
2	Isaiah 38:1–6; Matthew 8:5–13; Psalm 54
3	Isaiah 58:1–9; Matthew 4:43–48, 6:1–4; Psalm 26
4	Isaiah 58:9–14; Mark 6:47–56 and "Easter in the Early Church" (Chapter Three)
5	Ezekiel 34:11–16; Matthew 25:31–46; Psalm 83
6	Isaiah 55:6–11; Matthew 21:10–17; Psalm 89
7	Exodus 24:12–18; Matthew 12:38–50; First Letter
8	Ezekiel 18:1–9; Matthew 15:21–28; Psalm 16
9	Ezekiel 18:20–28; John 5:1–15; Psalm 85
10	Deuteronomy 26:12–19; 1 Thessalonians 5:14–23; Second Letter
11	Daniel 9:15–19; John 8:21–29; Psalm 69
12	1 Kings 17:8–16; Matthew 23:1–12; Psalm 54
13	Psalm 27; Matthew 20:17–28; Third Letter
14	Jeremiah 17:5–10; Luke 16:19–31; Psalm 78
15	Genesis 37:6–22; Matthew 21:33–46; Psalm 11
16	Genesis 27:6–39; Luke 1:11–32; Fourth Letter
17	2 Kings 5:1–15; Luke 4:23–30; Psalm 55
18	2 Kings 4:1–7; Matthew 18:15–22; Psalm 18
19	Exodus 20:12–24; Matthew 15:1–20; Fifth Letter
20	Jeremiah 7:1–7; Luke 4:38–44; Psalm 144
21	Exodus 17:2; Numbers 20:1–3; 6–13; John 4:5–42; Psalm 27
22	Daniel 13:1–9; 15–17; 19–30; 33–62; John 8:1–11; Sixth Letter

23 1 Kings 3:16–28; John 2:13–25; Psalm 30
24 Exodus 32:7–14; John 7:14–31; Psalm 43
25 Ezekiel 36:23–26; John 9:1–38; Seventh Letter
26 2 Kings 4:8–37; Luke 7:11–16; Psalm 73
27 1 Kings 17:17–24; John 11:1–45; Psalm 117
28 Isaiah 49:8–15; John 8:12–20; Eighth Letter
29 Jonah 3:1–10; John 7:32–39; Psalm 53
30 Daniel 14:29–42; John 7:1–13; Psalm 42
31 Leviticus 19:1–2, 11–19,25; John 10:22–38; Ninth Letter
32 Daniel 3:25,34–45; Luke 7:36–50; Psalm 95
33 Jeremiah 17:13–18; John 11:47–54; Psalm 34
34 Jeremiah 18:18–23
35 Isaiah 50:5–10; John 12:1–9; Psalm 102
36 Jeremiah 11:18–20; Mark 14:32–72; 15:1–46; Psalm 66
37 Isaiah 62:11; 63:1–7; Luke 22:39–71; Eleventh Letter
38 Isaiah 61:1–4,6,8,9; Luke 4:16–22; Psalm 88
39 Philippians 2:8,9; John 13:1–15; Psalm 47
40 Exodus 12:1–11; John 18,19; Twelfth Letter and Conclusion

QUESTIONS AND ANSWERS CONCERNING LENTEN PRACTICES

FASTING IN THE CHURCH[1]

Q. What do you mean by "fast days"?

A. Days set aside to humble ourselves before God, repressing the appetites of our bodies and turning our attention upon whatever matter the Lord has set before us.

Q. What is the nature of a fast?

A. In a strict sense, it implies total abstinence from all food and drink during the whole day. The ancient Christians often fasted from morning to evening and then ate sparingly of simple food. It appears that a fast period of several days often consisted of a string of days with such a simple meal at the end of each.

In a larger sense, fasting implies an abstinence from particular kinds of food, such as meat or wine, or a deferring of eating beyond the usual hours. In these cases as well, some self-denial of our bodily appetites is intended.

It seems that during periods of fasting in the ancient church, the daily simple meals, particularly during Lent, involved an abstinence from meat and wine. Such meals usually consisted of vegetables, grains, and legumes. They held to a cheap and plain diet at such times, without appetizing sauces or delicacies. Some held to a dry diet of nuts and similar foods, and some ate only bread and water.

[1]Partially adapted from Robert Nelson, *A Companion for the Festivals and Fasts* (London: T. Osborne, *et al.*, 1766).

Q. What are the reasons for Christian fasts?

A. For one thing, it is a proper means to express sorrow and grief. It is also an appropriate tool to help us turn our minds toward anything that is serious. We find ancient descriptions that suggest an almost universal use of fasting as a part of repentance, an act of humbling oneself before God. In the case of Jonah's encounter with the Ninevites (Jonah 3:5), we see that this was a concept they understood. There is, of course, Old Testament precedent for fasting (Ps. 69:10; Daniel 9:3).

Our Savior did not give us any specific commands to fast, but He did join it to almsgiving and prayer. His instructions about *how* to fast (Matt. 6:16–18) presuppose that it will be done. In that passage He indicates when a fast will be acceptable to God. On another occasion He expressly said that the time would come when His disciples would fast (Luke 5:35). When He tells of the Pharisee who boasted that he fasted twice each week, Jesus does not blame him for fasting but for boasting about it. (See also Luke 2:37; Acts 10:30; Acts 13:2.)

Q. Was fasting practiced in the ancient church?

A. There are several references:

a. Polycarp, bishop of Smyrna, wrote in a letter to the Philippians sometime before the middle of the second century:

> Therefore let us give up the vanity of the crowd and the false teachings and return to the word handed on to us from the beginning, being sober in prayer, and persevering in fasts, in our entreaties beseeching the all-seeing God to lead us not into temptation, as the Lord said: "The Spirit is willing but the flesh is weak."

b. In the *Didache*, a second-century document:

> But do not let your fasts fall on the same days as "the hypocrites" (Matt. 6:16ff.), who fast on Monday and Thursday. Rather you should fast on Wednesday and Friday" (8:1).

c. There is also material on fasting in the second-century *Shepherd of Hermas*, where the emphasis is on doing more than going through the motions of a fast.[2]

d. As time goes on and we have more writings available to examine, we find the pre-Easter fast practiced throughout Christendom. See especially the Festal Letters of Athanasius.

Q. When should we consider that a fast is undertaken for "spiritual" or "religious" purposes?

A. When it is undertaken to restrain the appetites of the body and to keep it under control so that we can devote ourselves to the Lord. Also, when we intend to humble ourselves before God under a sense of the magnitude of our sins. I would say that in some sense it can be so when we knowledgeably fast in order to make up for the fact that we have overindulged in those good things God gives us to enjoy, and have therefore put on weight that we should not have. Without doubt, the control of our bodily appetites is somehow related to our ability to place a true value on the happiness of the future life.

Q. What should we do if fasting hurts our health?

A. It might be that plain and simple food in smaller quantities would be suitable in such a case.

THE FORTY DAYS OF LENT

Q. What do you mean by Lent?

A. The word "Lent" comes from the old Saxon language and means "spring." You can see how it came to be associated in the English language with the spring fast observed during the period before the great festival of our Savior's resurrection.

[2]Jack Sparks, ed., *Apostolic Fathers* (Nashville: Thomas Nelson, 1978), pp. 210–13.

Q. Is there any way we can know that this fast is truly an ancient one in the church?

A. The testimonies are many. Irenaeus, who wrote no more than ninety years after the death of the apostle John and who studied under Polycarp (who had known that apostle and others), tells us that the fast was observed in his time just as it had been previously. At that time there was great variety in the length of the fast. There is no ancient data to be found contradicting the observance of a solemn fast before Easter. By the time of Athanasius in the fourth century, the period was definitely forty days.

Q. Why forty days?

A. No one can say for sure, although the association of the number "forty" with repentance, mourning, and preparation has much scriptural precedence (Gen. 7:4; Num. 14:34; Deut. 25:3; 9:9; 9:25; 1 Kings 19:8; Jonah 3:4; Matt. 4:2).

Q. What was the purpose of the ancient Lenten fast?

A. It was a time set apart as a proper season for:

1. Exercising self-control
2. Reminding us of the sufferings of Christ for us
3. Contributing to our public confession that He died for our salvation
4. Preparing ourselves to celebrate His resurrection with gladness and joy, participating in that Feast time as a sort of "first fruit" of the Marriage Supper of the Lamb.

Q. How did the ancient Christians observe the Lenten fast?

A. There was variety:

1. Some abstained from meat and wine through all of Lent.
2. Some fasted on particular days.
3. Some also cut out eggs and fruit, eating only vegetables and bread.
4. In Holy Week itself, some ate only bread and water and salt, or a dry diet of nuts, etc.

All was done, however, as the church directed, so that people knew what they should do and knew what leeway (in both directions) was permissible.

Q. But since the life of a Christian ought always to be under the lordship of Christ, isn't it rather contradictory to set aside such a time as Lent for this purpose?

A. We cannot keep everything in mind all the time. The seasons of the year give us regular times for self-control and self-examination, hope and rejoicing — all in the perspective of appropriate aspects of what the Lord has done for us. If all were fasting, we would perhaps think too much of our self-control. If all were feasting, we would perhaps grow spiritually fat and dull of hearing, learning only to indulge ourselves. It is very good that we have such a solemn season as Lent, when the command of our superiors, the provision of fit means to assist us, and the practice of devout Christians in all ages call us to sober thought concerning repentance and faith — yea, call us to holy and godly living.

ASH WEDNESDAY—
THE FIRST DAY OF LENT

Q. Why does the forty-day fast, called Lent, begin on Ash Wednesday?

A. Since the church has never fasted on Sundays, the period must begin forty-six days before Easter. Although we may actually fast only on certain days, we consider the whole period a fast—except for the Sundays. They remain celebrations of the Resurrection.

Q. Why is the day called "Ash" Wednesday?

A. It was a custom in the ancient church for those who were penitents to express their humiliation by dressing in sackcloth and covering themselves with ashes. By the sackcloth they ranked themselves among people in the lowest condition. The ashes reminded them of their mortality.

SCRIPTURE INDEX

Genesis
4:16 134
7:4 208
22:13 106
49:14 170
Exodus
8:26 157
12:2 179
12:7, 23 77
12:5 191–192
12:8, 9, 46 196
12:11 101
12:11–13 178
12:42 20
12:43 108
12:43–44 178
12:46 94
12:47 177
14 136
14:14 154
15:1 69, 76, 81, 176
16:3 191
19:3–7 178
19:8 177, 178
19:16 50
19:20 134
23:14 49
24:2 73
29:21 177
34:33–35 188
Leviticus
11:13 116
23:26 52
23:29 52
Numbers
8:7 177
9:2 70
10:1 49
10:9 49–50
10:10 50
14:34 208
*2:2 93
Deuteronomy
4:20 76, 157
4:24 73
6:4 149
6:7 153
9:3 73
9:9 208
9:25 208
13:1–3 172
16:1 100
*16:12 187
18:15 135, 180
25:3 208
26:5 21
28:66 135
1 Samuel
15:22 192

*Septuagint

1 Kings
8:51 157
12:32, 33 62
19:8 208
2 Kings
6:13–17 136
Esther
3:9 141
4:16 82
9:20–28 82
9:21 141
Job
1:21 168
2:7 134
7:1 167
*14:4 95
*40:8,9 167
Psalms
1:1,2 91, 153
2:1 135, 152
2:4 160
4:1 147
4:5 192
5:3 109
*7:3,4 181
9:15,16 153
9:17 116
12:6 73
14:1 155,193
14:7 48
16:3 51
17:3 168
17:15 120
18:29 76, 195
*18:45 135, 189
19:4 83, 158
19:14 153
23:4 33, 55
24:3–5 108
26:2 168
30:9 103
*31:7 176
32:9 61
33:1 105
Psalms (Cont.)
34:1 75
34:21 117
35:8 153
35:9 105
35:28 66
37:15 152
38:12 151
40:6 106
42:1 120
42:4 56, 107
43:3 140
43:4 134
44:17 75, 159
44:22 115
49:3 153
49:10 193
49:11 169
50:14 192
50:16 118
50:23 192
55:15 193
57:4 152
63:1,2 120–121
63:6 153
66:11 147
66:12 147
69:10 206
73:20 62
74:14 52
76:1 83
80:7 140
81:3 49, 70
*90:14 158
94:17 92
95:1 105, 158
97:1 82
100:4 134
101:6 134–135
104:4 73
104:25, 26 194
104:34 192
106:9 76
113–118 21

*Septuagint

Psalms (Cont.)
115:8 62
115:17, 18 117
116:12 92
116:13 92
116:15 92, 117
118:17 118
118:24 161
119:62 176
119:143 154
119:148 154
119:164 108
*120:5 147
124:6 141
*125:1 150, 153–154
132:15 120
136 38
137:1 82
141:2 192
143:5 153
150:6 107
Proverbs
1:5 194
4:1 60
5:3, 4 119
5:22 192
5:23 193
9:1–5 119–120
9:6 120
9:17 119
*9:18 119
10:3 120
11:26 72
12:11 72
13:13 108
15:19 72
15:28 118
*19:27 151
20:17 119
*24:9 193
*26:10 193
Ecclesiastes
3:1 48
10:8 152
Song of Solomon
8:1 48
Isaiah
1:2 135
1:11 188
1:12 189, 190
1:13 188
1:14 101, 188
2:3 108
*3:9, 10 152
3:9, 10 192
6:9, 10 62
7:14 180
11:1 76
11:5 76
22:13 65, 116
22:14 116
23:2 61
*26:10 116
38:18, 19 117–118
38:20 131–132
40:18 62
42:12 102
44:23 107
48:22 62, 71
49:8 49
49:13 107
50:6 138
53:4 37
53:5 106
53:7 55, 106
55:6, 7 149
58:5 51–52
57:4 188
59:3–5 151
59:9–11 151
66:3 190
Jeremiah
2:18 119
5:8 61
4:3 72
6:16 177
6:20 188
7:3, 4 189–190

*Septuagint

Jeremiah (Cont.)
7:18 189
7:21, 22 189
7:22 190, 191
7:23 191
7:34 62, 71, 189–190
9:2 155
17:10 167
20:9 74
20:12 167
25:10 104
48:10 73
Lamentations
3:27–32 169
4:6 136
Ezekiel
16:48 136
18:23, 32 74
Daniel
1–3 132
3:23–24 132
9:3 206
11:31 54–55
Hosea
6:6 192
Joel
2:15 51
Jonah
3:4 208
3:5 206
Nahum
1:15 54, 70, 100
2:1 54
Zechariah
8:19 180
Malachi
1:11 84, 158
3:3 168
4:2 48, 94
Matthew
4:2 208
4:10 134
5:6 120
5:8 117
Matthew (Cont.)
5:11, 12 159
5:22 154
5:28 154
6:16 206
6:16–18 206
7:15 38
7:25 150
8:1 206
9:13 192
10:22 73
11:29 63
12:34 193
12:43–45 72
13:8 133
13:22 150
13:52 153
15:3 64
15:19 193
15:22, 23 121
15:26 121
15:28 121–122
18:20 131
18:34 71
20:22, 23 92
21:19 104, 105
21:33 104
22:12 123
22:14 123
22:29 192
24:15 55
25:1–12 124
25:11 116
25:21 58, 61, 159
25:23 72
25:26–28 71
25:26–30 103
25:34 108, 134
26:2 37
26:17 83
26:28 82
26:26–28 84
26:38 105
26:65–68 102

*Septuagint

Matthew (Cont.)
28:20 176
Mark
4:17 194–195
4:20 74
4:35–41 194
10:28 177
Luke
1:1–4 65
2:37 206
3:7 61
5:35 206
6:49 195
10:19 82
12:36 94
12:40 33, 55
12:49 74
13:25 116
14:15 122–123
15:17, 18, 19 123
16:19 137
17 74
17:15–18 102
17:19 102
18:7 172
18:10 51
22:12–16 109
22:15 178
22:16 100
22:29, 30 122
22:31 108
23:28 160
23:43 92
24 74
24:5 77
John
1:1 149–150
1:9 74
1:29 177
4:14 161
4:34 52
5:46 189
6:4 101
6:35 124
John (Cont.)
6:48 118–119
6:48–51 120
6:51 119, 120, 137
6:53 52
6:54–57 202
6:68 124
7:17 155
7:37 37, 51, 90, 121, 179, 180
7:38 112, 121
7:39 158
7:46 180
8:56 106
9:28, 29 192
12:28 162
13:12–15 63
13:18 74
14:2 134
14:6 82, 177
14:11 140
16:33 171, 179
20:22 54, 158
Acts
8:30 193
10:30 206
13:2 206
Romans
1:22, 23, 28 62
1:28 168
2:21 60
2:23 51
3:31 180
5:3 171
5:3–5 75, 169
5:5 158
5:12, 18 160
5:14 92
6:3–11 115
6:5, 6 25
6:9 139
8:9–13 101
8:13 124
8:17, 18 170
8:23 56

*Septuagint

Romans (Cont.)
8:24, 25 146
8:35 130
8:37 128, 138, 167
8:38, 39 138
*9:3 181
10:4 179–80
11:23 105
12:12 154
13:7 104, 131
14:1 122, 135
14:2 133
16:18 156
1 Corinthians
1:24 48
2:2 196
2:8 153, 192
2:9 56
3:1 122
3:2 133
3:12 169
4:4 146
4:16 60
4:21 14
5:7 22, 35–36, 46, 51, 66, 71, 76, 101, 118, 131, 141, 160, 172, 176, 180, 187
5:8 33, 46, 51, 55, 100
6:13 116
6:17 150
6:20 102
7:7 147
9:22 148
9:27 169
10:4 150
10:16 27
11:1 00, 138, 147
11:2 63
11:27 95
12:13 26
13:9, 12 146
14:25 63
15:12–57 66
1 Corinthians (Cont.)
15:53 103, 160
15:55 107
2 Corinthians
1:22 56, 181
2:16 91
3:12–18 188
3:17 55
4:10 115, 124
4:13, 14 115
4:17 170
5:5 181
5:10 134
5:13–15 102
6:2 49
6:1, 2 102
6:14 118
6:17 157
7:6 70
12:4 146
12:9 167
12:10 168
12:21 147
Galatians
1:9 59, 65
2:20 89, 93, 117
3:23, 24 188
3:27 26
4:10 70–71, 101
4:11 101
5:22 103
5:25 115
Ephesians
1:3 187
1:13, 14 181
2:4, 5 132
2:19 146
4:22–24 33, 55
4:24 63
5:14 116
5:30 27
6:12 50
6:14 146
6:15 33, 55, 76, 179

*Septuagint

Philippians
1:29 166
2:7–11 102
3:13 95
3:14 171
3:15 146
3:17–20 117
4:5 33, 55
4:6 76
4:13 138
Colossians
1:28 169
1:15 179
2:12 26
3:4 123
3:5 115, 117, 118, 121
1 Thessalonians
5:16–18 157
5:17 66, 76
5:18 66, 195
5:19 73
1 Timothy
1:15 65
1:19 64
2:7 60, 148
4:6 52, 122
4:7 168
4:7, 8 154, 156
4:12 63
4:14 73
4:15 150
6:12 156
2 Timothy
1:13 122
2:8 66, 94, 150
2:16, 17 156
2:18 63, 156
2:19 145, 157
3:12 156
3:13 171
3:14 150, 156
4:2 48
Hebrews
2:14 66, 172
3:6 73
Hebrews (Cont.)
5:13 122
5:14 133, 195
6:18 190
9:10 49, 191
9:13 177
9:26 179
10:1 191
10:24 166
10:29 123
11:6 121, 149
11:16 118
11:17 106
12:23 107
12:24 33, 55
12:29 73
James
1:2, 3 171
1:14 171
1:27 47
4:8–10 185
1 Peter
1:7 165, 168
1:13 76
2:9 22
2:21–23 63
2:23 138
2 Peter
1:4 95, 175
1 John
4:1 39
Books of the Apocrypha:
Ecclesiasticus
15:9 118
18:17 192
Judith
9 82
13:8 82
Song of the Three Children
23–28 132
Wisdom
1:4, 5 73
2:12 152, 192
7:27 48, 133

*Septuagint

SUBJECT AND NAME INDEX

Abel, 55
Ablavius (Praefect of the Praetorium), 80, 84
Abraham, 14, 98, 105, 106, 195
Adam, 92, 160
Against the Heathen, 29
Alexander, Bishop, 13, 28, 29, 31, 33, 64
Alexandria, 13, 28, 31, 32, 33, 35, 36, 37, 38, 39, 40, 80, 130, 158, 164
Ambrose, St., 22
Angelic, 14
Angels, 53, 73, 74 (the devil's), 77, 107, 108, 113, 122, 124, 136, 138, 141
Antichrists, 113, 137
Antioch, 36
Apollinaris, 40
Apology Against The Arians, 37
Apostle(s), 19, 38, 63, 65, 74, 83, 101, 108, 130, 148, 177
apostolic behavior, 63
apostolic custom, 142
apostolic injunction, 72
apostolic tradition, 66
apostolic writings, 149
Arian(s), 13, 32, 33, 34, 35, 37, 38, 40, 59, 128, 139, 140, 141, 144, 145, 150, 156, 159, 164, 166, 184
Arianism, 13, 38
Arius, 13, 31, 35
Archdeacon, 13, 31, 32
Arsenius, 34
Ash Wednesday, 209
Athanasius, St., 13, 14, 16, 17, 18, 23, 28, 29, 30, 31, 32, 33, 34, 35, 36, 37, 38, 39, 40, 41, 46, 58, 59, 68, 69, 80, 88, 98, 99, 112, 113, 128, 129, 130, 144, 158, 164, 174, 178, 184, 187, 188, 197, 201, 207, 208
atonement, 52
Azariah, 132
Basil of Seleucia, 26
baptism, 22, 23, 25, 26, 29, 174
baptismal liturgy, 28, 29
bread, unleavened with Passover, 20, 21, 104, 179
Bread, unleavened (Christ), 122, 189
bread, unleavened of sincerity and truth, 33, 55, 76, 100
Bultmann, Rudolph, 59
Burgess, Henry Rev., 16

Caiaphas, 102
Cain, 159
Callinicus, 85
Catholic Church, 32, 94, 118, 158
celebration, 17, 18, 20, 22, 23, 24, 25, 37, 45, 46, 48, 49, 58, 80, 91, 107, 166, 172, 177, 181, 195, 209
Chrysostom, John, 24, 200, 201
Church, the 13, 14, 16, 17, 18, 19, 22, 23, 24, 25, 26, 27, 37, 46, 65, 81, 94, 98, 104, 107, 118, 129, 132, 133, 141, 156, 164, 166, 184, 187, 200, 201, 205, 206, 208, 209
church(es), 28, 29, 30, 31, 33, 34, 37, 58, 60, 66, 80, 88, 107, 108, 131
Christian Science, 59
clergy, 29
Cleopas, 74
Constans, 35, 36
Constantine, 34, 35, 68, 80, 84
Constantine II, 35
Constantinople, 35, 80, 128
Constantius, 35, 36, 37, 39, 158, 184
Corinth, 22, 60
Council of Nicaea (325 A.D.), 13, 15, 16, 31, 32, 39
Creator, 149, 160
Creed (of Nicaea), 32, 39
cross, 18, 24, 30, 37, 91, 186
Daniel, 53, 98, 108
David, 62, 66, 75, 98, 108, 135, 150, 176, 181, 192
deacon, 9, 31
Deity, 15, 63
Deliverer, 100, 101
devil, 25, 32, 39, 52, 64, 66, 74, 80, 82, 83, (kingdom of), 94, 101, 108, 113, 134, 138, 140, 172
Didache, 206
Diocletian, emperor, 29
disciples, 37, 63, 65, 72, 74, 84, 92, 104, 121, 123, 153, 156, 168, 178, 192, 194, 195, 206
discipline, 23, 29, 76, 116, 200
Door (Christ), 174, 176
Easter, 16, 17, 18, 23, 33, 46, 48, 58, 60, 66, 70, 76, 83, 93, 95, 100, 107, 109, 124, 141, 142, 144, 159, 161, 172, 181, 196, 200, 201, 207, 208, 209
  Feast, 16, 37, 48, 66, 76, 77, 81, 88, 112, 115
  festival, 41, 70, 196
  Letter, 33, 35, 36, 37, 41, 46, 58, 68, 80, 141, 164
  Week, 56
Egypt, 19, 20, 21, 22, 23, 24, 28, 31, 33, 34, 37, 39, 73, 94, 100, 109, 119, 136, 141, 157, 172, 189, 190, 191
Elijah, 53, 176
Elisha, 136–137
Emmanuel, 150
Epistles, 22, 27
Esther, 82, 141
Esau, 135, 136
eternal life, 27, 56, 112, 124, 136, 154, 156, 161, 170, 202
eternity, 16
Eucharist, 23, 27
  Great, 24, 46, 80, 201
Eucharistic meal, 27
Eudaemon, 85
Eusebius of Caesarea, 98
Eusebius of Nicomedia, 145, 158
Eve, 64

exile, 4, 33, 35, 36, 37, 40, 41, 128
Exodus (from Egypt), 20, 21, 24
faith, 14, 15, 16, 18, 19, 26, 29, 36, 60, 63, 64, 72, 74, 76, 82, 93, 102, 106, 115, 121, 122, 129, 132, 134, 139, 144, 145, 148, 150, 153, 155, 156, 157, 158, 159, 164, 165, 166, 167, 168, 171, 174, 175, 180, 183, 184, 185, 188, 190, 194, 195, 201, 209
fast, 21, 23, 33, 41, 46, 47, 51, 53, 56, 66, 76, 77, 80, 84, 88, 90, 93, 95, 109, 124, 142, 144, 161, 172, 180, 181, 196, 200, 201, 203, 205, 206, 207, 208, 209
  Holy, 109
  Lenten, 109
fasting, 24, 46, 47, 49, 50, 51, 53, 82, 99, 107, 109, 181, 196, 200, 201, 205, 206, 207, 209
Father, 19, 23, 30, 31, 32, 49, 53, 56, 66, 77, 82, 91, 95, 102, 108, 110, 113, 122, 124, 125, 134, 139, 140, 142, 152, 158, 159, 160, 161, 172, 179, 181, 187, 190, 197, 202
Fathers, church, 15, 16, 18, 25, 26, 65, 66, 129, 130, 142
father(s), 21, 60, 112, 120, 123, 151, 189, 190
feast, 16, 21, 22, 24, 33, 46, 49, 50, 51, 54, 55, 56, 62, 66, 70, 81, 82, 83, 88, 90, 100, 104, 105, 107, 108, 117, 123, 124, 141, 167, 174, 176, 178, 180, 187, 189, 197, 208
Feast, 33, 35, 36, 37, 41, 58, 60, 61, 70, 76, 80, 81, 82, 83, 84, 90, 91, 93, 95, 100, 101, 104, 106, 108, 109, 112, 117, 118, 123, 125, 129, 130, 131, 141, 144, 145, 157, 158, 159, 160, 166, 171, 172, 174, 175, 176, 177, 178, 179, 180, 185, 187, 195, 196, 197, 200, 201
  Eternal, 177
  Great, 51, 90, 201
  "Feast of Weeks", 56
festal letters, 16–17, 33, 36, 128, 164, 174, 184, 187, 207
festal song, 81
festival, 18, 23, 24, 49, 66, 80, 82, 98, 99, 107, 117, 177, 181, 187, 196, 207
  Great, 22
  Resurrection, 99
Gamaliel, Rabbi, 21
Gentile(s), 19, 118, 148
God, 13, 14, 16, 20, 21, 22, 26, 27, 30, 31, 32, 33, 35, 38, 46, 48, 49, 50, 51, 52, 53, 55, 56, 60, 61, 62, 63, 64, 65, 68, 70, 71, 72, 73, 74, 75, 76, 80, 82, 83, 84, 88, 90, 91, 92, 93, 94, 95, 97, 98, 99, 100, 101, 102, 104, 106, 107, 108, 112, 113, 115, 116, 117, 118, 119, 120, 121, 128, 129, 131, 132, 133, 134, 135, 136, 137, 138, 139 140, 141, 145, 146, 147, 148, 149, 150, 154, 155, 156, 157, 158, 164, 165, 166, 167, 168, 169, 170, 171, 172, 174, 176, 177, 178, 179, 181, 184, 185, 187, 188, 189, 190, 191, 192, 193, 195, 196, 197, 200, 205, 206, 207
Godhead, 15, 30, 65, 144, 162
"Golden Decade," 37

good works, 23, 76, 145
Gospel, 22, 55, 60, 64, 65, 66, 76, 84, 103, 118, 120, 137, 146, 150, 179, 196
grace, 72, 73, 74, 82, 90, 91, 93, 99, 100, 101, 103, 110, 115, 123, 124, 133, 135, 139, 147, 177, 185
Hananiah, 132
Harnack, Adolph, 59
heaven, 30, 32, 41, 53, 61, 66, 91, 98, 100, 106, 107, 108, 116, 117, 119, 120, 122, 123, 137, 146, 159, 160, 167, 170, 176, 185, 189, 195, 197, 201
hell, 58, 61, 92, 112, 116, 117, 180, 185
Helper, 102, 139, 153
herbs, 20, 21
heresy/heresies, 13, 14, 15, 31, 40, 57, 64, 192
heretics, 35, 36, 58, 59, 75, 76, 88, 93, 104, 118, 128, 139, 145, 159, 164, 166, 190, 193
Hezekiah, 117, 131
Hieracammon, Geloeus (Eulozius), 85
holiday(s), 20, 58, 62, 82, 90, 107, 117
Holy Day, 17, 20, 46, 58, 88, 91, 112, 129, 196
Holy Spirit, 15, 32, 33, 38, 52, 54, 55, 56, 66, 72, 73, 77, 91, 113, 116, 125, 151, 158, 174, 192, 197
Holy Week, 23, 77, 172
Hymeneus, 64, 156, 157, 194
hypostasis, 39
incarnate, 14, 101, 139, 140
incarnation, 40, 103, 148, 174
The Incarnation of the Word of God, 29
Isaac, 14, 98, 105, 106
Isaiah, 49, 55, 106, 135, 180, 188, 189
Ision, 85
Issachar, 170, 171
Israel, 20, 21, 22, 23, 49, 50, 51, 54, 70, 73, 82, 83, 84, 94, 98, 107, 109, 170, 177
Iranaeus of Lyons, 27, 208
Jacob, 14, 108, 135
James, St., 171
Jehovah's Witnesses, 59
Jeremiah, 73, 147, 155, 177, 189
Jericho, 158
Jerusalem, 20, 35, 41, 53, 54, 75, 76, 80, 83, 84, 94, 99, 109, 154, 170, 177, 190, 196
Jesse, 76
Jesus Christ, 13, 15, 16, 17, 18, 19, 20, 22, 24, 25, 26, 27, 28, 29, 30, 31, 31, 34, 36, 40, 46, 48, 51, 52, 53, 56, 59, 60, 62, 63, 66, 70, 74, 76, 79, 80, 83, 84, 87, 89, 91, 93, 94, 95, 98, 101, 102, 103, 104, 110, 112, 113, 115, 117, 118, 119, 122, 125, 128, 129, 130, 131, 132, 133, 136, 137, 138, 139, 140, 141, 142, 145, 146, 147, 148, 150, 152, 156, 159, 160, 161, 164, 165, 166, 167, 169, 170, 171, 172, 173, 174, 175, 176, 177, 179, 180, 181, 184, 187, 188, 195, 196, 197, 201, 208
  body of, 26, 27, 80, 84, 89, 103, 160, 174, 202
  blood of, 27, 33, 52, 55, 80, 84, 89, 90, 91, 98, 103, 122, 174, 202

Jesus Christ (Cont.)
flesh, 52, 103, 133, 174, 179, 202
Jews, 19, 20, 21, 25, 26, 37, 53, 54, 56, 64, 75, 88, 93, 98, 101, 106, 118, 119, 135, 136, 140, 150, 152, 159, 160, 174, 177, 184, 187, 188, 189, 192, 193, 194
Jewish, 19, 21, 22, 54, 83, 105, 178
Job, 75, 95, 134, 136, 167, 168, 195
John of Damascus, 113, 149, 177, 208
Jonah, 206
Joseph, 135, 195
Jovian, emperor, 40
Judaea, 53, 82, 83
Judaism, 19
Judas, 74, 108, 123, 194
Julian, emperor, 39, 40
King, 19, 136, 141
Kingdom of heaven, 27, 30, 65, 92, 95, 108, 109, 113, 122, 123, 124, 134, 136, 147, 153, 169, 170, 174, 181
Lamb, 55, 79, 95
Passover, 22, 80, 174
Paschal, 22, 196
Marriage Supper of, 208
lamb, 20, 21, 25, 53, 55, 82, 84, 104, 105, 106, 141, 189, 190
blood of, 20, 82
Law, 19, 50, 51, 53, 54, 73, 104, 108, 117, 135, 146, 148, 179, 184, 189, 190, 191, 192
law(s), 33, 55, 91, 92, 94, 104, 118, 136, 149, 155, 177, 178
Lazarus, 137
Leader, 177
Lent, 201, 203, 205, 207, 208, 209
Life, 118, 152, 174
Light, 179
liturgy, 28, 178
Lord, 13, 19, 20, 21, 24, 26, 27, 30, 32, 33, 34, 35, 37, 41, 46, 48, 49, 50, 51, 52, 55, 56, 60, 61, 62, 63, 64, 66, 68, 69, 71, 72, 73, 74, 75, 76, 77, 81, 82, 83, 84, 88, 89, 90, 91, 92, 93, 94, 95, 98, 100, 101, 102, 103, 104, 105, 106, 107, 108, 109, 110, 112, 113, 115, 116, 117, 118, 120, 121, 122, 123, 124, 125, 127, 130, 131, 132, 134, 136, 137, 138, 139, 140, 141, 142, 144, 145, 146, 147, 148, 149, 150, 152, 153, 154, 155, 157, 158, 159, 160, 161, 167, 168, 169, 170, 171, 172, 176, 177, 178, 179, 180, 181, 185, 186, 187, 189, 190, 191, 192, 193, 194, 195, 196, 197, 201, 205, 207, 209
Luke, 65
marriage, 50
Marcarius, 30
martyrdom, 30
martyrs, 165, 168
Master, 63, 194
Matthew, 150
Maximin, emperor, 30
Messiah, 19, 22, 106
Mishael, 132
Mishna, the, 22
Melito of Sardis, 18, 19, 25
Moses, 20, 41, 49, 52, 53, 54, 69, 73, 76, 82, 92, 94, 98, 100, 101, 108, 134, 135, 149, 172, 176, 177, 178, 179, 180, 188,

Moses (Cont.)
189, 190, 192, 193
Mormonism, 59
Nazianzen, Gregory St., 14
New Covenant, 82 (blood of), 84 (promise)
Nisan (Jewish month of Passover), 21
offering(s), 30, 52, 54, 89, 106, 117, 140, 188, 189, 190, 191
Old Testament, 49, 68, 187, 206
One Holy Catholic and Apostolic Church, 196
Only-Begotten, 104
orthodox, 36, 37
orthodox doctrine, 13
orthodox faith, 64
orthodoxy, 14, 34, 139
partakers, 27, 109
partakers of Christ, 63, 73, 95, 121, 160, 175
Pascha, 18, 19, 23, 24, 26
Paschal celebration, 23, 25
Paschal sacrifice, 21
Passover, 19, 20, 21, 22, 37, 46, 51, 66, 70, 76, 79, 80, 82, 83, 84, 88, 89, 90, 94, 95, 98, 99, 100, 101, 104, 105, 108, 109, 118, 141, 157, 160, 172, 174, 175, 176, 177, 178, 184, 187, 189, 196, 201
pastor, 14
Paul, Apostle, 22, 25, 26, 27, 30, 33, 46, 48, 49, 50, 51, 52, 55, 59, 60, 62, 63, 64, 65, 66, 70, 72, 73, 74, 75, 76, 89, 91, 93, 94, 98, 101, 102, 103, 105, 133, 138, 139, 141, 145, 146, 147, 148, 150, 154, 156, 157, 160, 167, 168, 176, 179, 181, 187, 188, 190, 195
penitence, 47, 196
Pentecost, 24, 56, 66, 77, 84, 95, 109, 125, 142, 161, 172, 181, 196
Peri Pascha, 19
persecution, 29, 36, 58, 72, 130, 137, 151, 154, 156, 164, 166, 167, 168, 169, 195
Peter, St., 22
Peter, bishop of Alexandria, 30
Pharaoh, king of Egypt, 20, 25, 81, 82, 94, 176, 178
Pharisees, 51, 180, 193, 206
Philetus, 156, 194
Pilate, 102
Pistus, 36
Polycarp, bishop of Smyrna, 206, 208
prayer(s), 16, 17, 21, 23, 24, 49, 66, 70, 71, 76, 88, 90, 91, 95, 98, 109, 121, 131, 149, 154, 158, 166, 176, 181, 190, 192, 195, 196, 201, 206
presbyter(s), 9, 31, 130
promised land, 49, 136
psalms, 21, 23, 24, 41, 70, 75, 105, 134, 135, 141
Redeemer, 102, 114, 123, 139, 140, 153, 159
redemption, 16, 22, 23, 24, 25, 26, 27, 34, 37, 200, 201
resurrection, 18, 22, 25, 26, 27, 30, 64, 66, 80, 95, 107, 156, 160, 194, 200, 207, 208, 209
Resurrection Letter(s), 17, 18
Rome, 36, 144, 164, 166
Sabellius, 14–15
sacrifice(s), 20, 21, 22, 25, 46, 51, 53, 54, 66, 71, 83, 84, 90, 98, 101, 104, 105, 106, 120, 141, 157, 158, 160, 172, 175, 176,

Sacrifice(s) (Cont.)
184, 187, 188, 189, 190, 191, 192, 201
Saducees, 64
saint(s), 41, 52, 53, 60, 61, 63, 66, 75, 84, 92, 95, 105, 107, 108, 117, 118, 120, 122, 123, 134, 136, 139, 146, 147, 151, 154, 157, 158, 167, 168, 170, 176, 181, 195, 201
salvation, 14, 22, 31, 32, 34, 40, 48, 49, 76, 91, 92, 94, 103, 105, 107, 128, 131, 132, 134, 141, 147, 166, 171, 179, 208
Samuel, 54, 147, 176, 192
Satan, 134
Saul, 135, 147, 192
Savior, 33, 39, 48, 49, 50, 51, 53, 54, 55, 56, 63, 65, 74, 76, 80, 82, 83, 90, 91, 94, 98, 102, 105, 106, 108, 112, 113, 115, 117, 121, 124, 129, 133, 135, 138, 139, 149, 154, 158, 160, 161, 171, 175, 177, 180, 185, 187, 194, 206, 207
Schleiermacher, F.E.D., 59
Scripture(s), 21, 23, 24, 29, 30, 31, 39, 49, 53, 59, 64, 68, 69, 70, 73, 80, 90, 95, 112, 121, 133, 134, 135, 139, 140, 150, 152, 160, 164, 170, 178, 180, 181, 184, 188, 189, 190, 192, 201
season(s), 24, 33, 45, 47, 48, 49, 55, 60, 66, 70, 76, 83, 93, 94, 98, 100, 109, 130, 142, 157, 161, 172, 187, 208, 209
Serapian, bishop of Thumuis, 164
Shepherd, 33, 55, 174, 176, 149
Shepherd of Hermas, 26, 207
sin(s), 14, 24, 25, 33, 37, 52, 55, 61, 73, 74, 76, 80, 88, 92, 99, 101, 105, 106, 107, 113, 116, 117, 118, 119, 124, 132, 134, 136, 138, 141, 150, 151, 152, 157, 160, 177, 185, 193, 207
Smith-Payne, Miss, 16
Solomon, 48, 60, 133, 193
Son, 15, 19, 23, 30, 31, 32, 36, 40, 49, 61, 62, 65, 71, 82, 91, 95, 102, 103, 104, 106, 112, 118, 124, 132, 139, 140, 144, 150, 156, 159, 174, 188, 191, 194
Spirit, 26, 36, 55, 61, 62, 68, 70, 73, 91, 103, 115, 118, 123, 124, 131, 133, 134, 135, 153, 158, 181, 192, 193, 206
spirit(s), 39, 40, 72, 73, 91, 101, 115, 122, 150, 153, 157, 166, 167, 184, 196, 200
Sun of Righteousness, 48, 94
Table of the Lord, 24, 88, 122, 124, 174, 175
tabernacle, 41
Theophilus, 65
Three Persons, 14, 15
Timothy, 48, 63, 122, 148, 150, 154, 155
Titus, 148
Trinity, 15
trumpet, 46, 49, 50, 51, 55, 63, 70, 105, 187
Truth, 83, 179
Unification Church, 59
unity, 14, 15, 39, 158, 196, 200
Valens, emperor, 40
Valentinia, emperor, 40
Virgin Mary, 65, 139, 180
virginity, 50
virgins, 50, 124, 133

Way, 174, 176, 177
Wierwille (The Way International), 59
wine, 21, 55, 120, 149, 171, 174, 205, 208
Wisdom, 31, 48, 62, 119, 120, 133
Wisdom, book of, 73, 152
Word, 15, 24, 27, 31, 32, 40, 53, 61, 65, 71, 74, 82, 92, 95, 101, 103, 104, 118, 121, 132, 133, 149, 152, 157, 159, 171, 174, 176, 177, 178, 179, 190, 191, 192, 194, 195, 196
worship, 23, 41, 70, 75, 98, 101, 104, 125, 150, 157, 158, 172